Chuck — Keep up .
good work — you are niqw a bow
PC

BORN
AGAIN

I hope this account of
my Experiences will

encourage You

God Bless You

Inrly

GAL. 2:20

Testimonial from Chuck Colson, Nixon Administration,
Author of the book Born Again

Mr. Colson wrote above testimonial prior to publication

ISBN: 978-1-7329040-5-7

POLITICAL
CORRECTNESS
IS TOTAL BS

(4TH EDITION)

HOW FAR LEFT ACTIVISTS, JUDICIAL MISCONDUCT AND POLITICAL CORRUPTION IS RUINING AMERICA

CHARLES S. TOGIAS

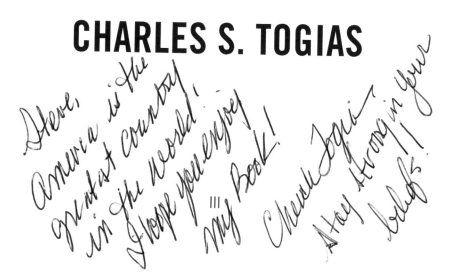

TABLE OF CONTENTS

Preface

During my many successful years in the advertising business, it has been my experience, that to effectively promote a product or communicate a message you need to apply both reach and frequency. Reach is the number of people who hear the message and frequency is the number of times they hear it. Chapter after chapter of my book I use frequency to ensure that my reader will understand my message. At times, I may sound redundant when discussing the far left and political and judicial systems but I do so to ensure clarity of message. I want to make it clear as to who is ruining our country.

In my book, Political Correctness is BS; I examine the effect that the far left politically correct activists, lawyers, and politicians are having on our society. I challenge their secular and non-traditional values and reveal their distorted misleading agendas. They are anti-Judeo-Christian traditional values and consider organized religion as archaic and foolish as well as attacking and trying to rewrite our Constitution. Both are the reason for America's greatness!

The far-left has a humanistic value system, which rejects anything related to God. They are the minority in our country trying to impose their agenda. Conforming to this doctrine just to avoid a confrontation is to give away your ability to think as an individual and replace it with a group-think mentality. I refuse to do that.

To complicate matters they use our judicial and political systems to challenge our traditions and they have been effective at getting legislation passed that helps give credibility to this distorted ideology. The majority no longer rules in America. Because of our nation's weak leadership, our country is being ruled by lobbyists and far-left activist groups. In my opinion having this type of weak, indecisive leadership will eventually lead to our nation's demise.

My book is controversial in its candor because I discuss subjects such as immigration, profiling, terrorism, religion, racism, abortion and much more. My conclusions are from what I consider a logical, commonsense approach and not from an activist self-serving idealistic approach.

I discuss that our society consists of two types of people with different mentalities. The protected (those that are kept safe) and the protectors (those whose job it is to keep society safe). Both, for the most part, are sincere and eager to identify our country's problems. The problem, as I see it, lies in their solutions. Identifying a problem is easy finding solutions that alleviate the problem, is much harder especially if you're idealistic.

The PC are protected and often very idealistic, because many of them are lawyers or influenced by the judicial process and their views on civil rights and civil liberties are non-negotiable. They believe that torture or profiling of America's enemies should never be an option no matter how valuable the information gathered or how many lives it would save. Illegal wiretapping is frowned upon for any reason. They view the world and our enemies from a safe distance and never personally engage in physical battles. Their idealism sounds very humane but will it lead to a peaceful outcome or to our eventual destruction? Idealism and logic are often in conflict with each other!

The protectors feel that they are more realistic in their assessment of our world. They have to be physically ready to engage the criminal element in the battle to protect society. They view torture as a necessary means to save lives. They believe that civil rights apply to only those who are not prepared to kill innocent victims. They view life differently because they have to be ready to fight tyranny in the trenches. I believe for the most part realism tries to seek a logical conclusion!

The far left in our country is the epitome of the PC protected. They hail former Cuban leader Fidel Castro as a liberator and former President George W. Bush as a killer of women and children, worse than the devil. When they communicate these beliefs they have no credibility with anyone with a shred of common sense. Their agenda is so distorted that they have lost touch with reality.

The American Civil Liberties Union (ACLU), which is, in my opinion, the greatest ally of the criminal defense attorney and the criminal is their point of reference. The secular ACLU will defend the civil rights of the criminal to the exclusion of the victim. They are intellectual bullies who spout anti-traditional values.

My book Political Correctness is BS is a commonsense, realistic view of our world through my life experiences. I feel we should base our system or culture on how society has benefited in an ethical and moral sense from the decisions our leaders have rendered. Truth, ethics, and morals should be our litmus test and applied to everything in our culture.

When we see our schools failing, our judicial system more

interested in following procedures than truth, our politicians compromising their values, and our communities in disarray because of misguided leadership, we should focus our efforts on finding solutions to these problems, not denying that the problems exist.

We as Americans must get our heads out of the sand and confront today's most important issues. When you read my book, you may be surprised by the way I view some of our most controversial topics and maybe even more surprised by my solutions. I feel if we would truthfully address these issues logically, without any self-serving politically motivated agenda, our society would benefit. Instead of making excuses and giving into the loudest activist groups, we should stand strong for our Constitution, Judeo-Christian values, truth, ethics, and morals.

When you start with a false premise, you will end up with a wrong conclusion. As I stated the PC protected the view of the world and its problems are idealistic. They are more interested in identifying problems and less interested in logical solutions.

My book looks at the problems of our society and defines them very honestly not worrying about being politically correct. Therefore, I feel my solutions will be beneficial to help eradicate these problems not just identify them.

I know some will not agree with me and that is OK. I am a Vietnam veteran and I am in the protector, realistic camp. I try to view the world in a positive and truthful manner. My book is about idealism versus realism. I am on the side of reality.

Exposing Americas Left and Media Bias-When will it stop!!

I did not know whether to name this mini-chapter **The Ukraine Investigation on President Trump or Washington and the main stream media BS at its worst.** I had to add this commentary and again had to revise my book and add a 4th edition to my book Political Correctness is BS. Every day I find Washington DC with the help of the main stream media, to be so corrupt and manipulative that it is impossible for anyone who is principle centered, as I believe most Americans are, to believe or condone this hypocrisy.

Example: When they found nothing in the perceived Russian conspiracy they came up with a reason to investigate the Ukraine. Let's review the Ukraine controversy and determine if those pointing the finger at President Trump and accusing him of pressuring Ukraine's President Volodymyr Zelensky, yet to be proven, asking him to investigate Hunter Biden's role in Ukraine politics would be justified. Hunter Biden the supposedly expert consultant hired by the Ukraine, has no knowledge of the business he was consulting and does not speak the language. Hunter was paid $83,000 dollars per month. Since Hunter had no idea of the business he was consulting and could not speak the language why was he hired? Also why doesn't Joe Biden have to answer this question since he was Vice-President of the United States when this occurred? Could this be a case of Washington/media hypocrisy?

Yet our mainstream media never wonders why. I wonder if they would have questioned President Trump and his administration if one of Trump's children, with the same business credentials, was hired and paid this amount while he was serving in office. The media now is in a complete frenzy because they say President Trump wanted Ukraine to look into the Hunter Biden matter. In fact, it's now the main reason the impeachment investigation has continued. I say if Mr. Trump did not want Ukraine to look into this matter that is a dereliction of duty and should be investigated! Of course, I am not a Washington insider so my intentions would be questioned by these swamp rats!

If President Trump did not question this criminal arm twisting I for one would be very disappointed. The mainstream media along with the far-left socialist wackos made me become a great supporter of our President. I had great difficulty supporting our President when he was first running, as I indicated in my book and now I love him. My standard for excellence in a business or with political leaders is a performance, not BS. Are the voters who hired him benefitting from the decisions he has made? Let's take a look: Lowest unemployment for Afro-Americans, Hispanic-Americans, Asian-Americans ever and the average household income has increased dramatically. Also, the stock market is surging! Americans are profiting greatly under this President yet the self-serving Democrats and the media say nothing. That speaks volumes to me. I once thought our politicians worked for us and based their success on our success. What a joke! I really believe as I stated in my book, the mainstream media and far-left democrats would be cheering in the streets if we suffered a depression under this President. Remember many on the left in Washington DC serve themselves not we the people who voted them in. This is a proven fact when we see many in Congress become millionaires while the districts they serve are in shambles!! Term limits anyone?

I want to say that I have great respect for anyone that is principle-centered and that means looking at a situation objectively whether you agree with it or not. Alan Dershowitz is someone that I did not like during the O.J. Simpson trial. Mr. Dershowitz seemed determined to free someone who I believed and most Americans believed was guilty. But my opinion of him has changed dramatically with his objective commentary regarding President Trump and the far left witch hunt. Mr. Dershowitz has expressed great clarity regarding this matter and although he is on the left he is very objective and I respect him for that. Mr. Dershowitz has proven to be principle-centered!

With the insanity in Washington and the Press biased, I stated that I felt obligated to continue to reveal the insanity! This is the reason for my 4th Edition. The problem is will it ever end? Many politicians I consider hoodlums in three-piece suits!

I want to close this chapter by repeating that I as an American citizen want the Ukraine to investigate the Biden's whether President Trump has requested it or not. Not to call the Biden's out for this injustice is the same as not investigating horrible Hillary for her 30,000 destroyed emails. Our countries future as a democratic republic hinges on truth, not selective outrage. These far-left con-artists will look under a magnifying glass at those they oppose while turning a blind eye on the corruption that will benefit them and their party! Washington DC has again revealed itself as a self-serving group of con artists and finger pointers!

We as a nation must stand for the truth and defeat this far-left socialist tyranny!! They want to violate and change our Judeo-Christian principles and our Constitution in favor of an anti-God government!! America will never recover if this far-left corrupt insanity is not defeated!! Hope you enjoy my book!

God Bless America!!

What they are saying

"Finally, someone has peeled back the PC veneer and exposed it for what it really is!!!!! Togias has done a masterful job of dissecting the impact of PC on every aspect of our society and culture. He has left no stone unturned and wasn't afraid to raise the issues that we all know are out there, but few will ever utter.

You can't walk away from reading this book without having a sense of relief that one citizen has said what we have all thought on many occasions. It's a cathartic read that you can't put down. Some of the passages are straight forward and in Your Face! But there are also a cornucopia of great messages and pragmatic solutions.

Don't expect a commentary – this fellow has put a huge stake in the ground and you won't be left wondering where he stands.

Get ready for the Truth!!!!

Thanks Chuck, I admire the power of your convictions!!!"

— Bill Marino, Former Telecom Senior Executive and Business Entrepreneur

"To say that PC is BS is an interesting read would be an understatement. It is actually a wake-up call for all of us that are tired of "political correctness' and do nothing. The book makes you think about what is right and wrong. It is a reality check about our society.

Chuck points out that if you even dare question their

position you are criticized, ridiculed and tagged as a bigot or racist. He draws the conclusion that because the majority of us, who know what is right, say nothing and the minority view is imposed on all of us.

You may not agree with some of Chuck's thoughts but he sure makes you think about what will happen if we continue to be complacent. He is right, PC is BS."

— **Ken Henson Retired Executive AT&T**

"I feel that Chuck Togias, although not "politically correct" in writing this book, has presented in a very concise way most of the reasons why our country is in the state that it is in today. While the book is an easy read, the content will also easily get your dander up and hopefully encourage you to do something and make a difference like Mr. Togias."

— **Charles Haskell, MBA, CPA Business Executive**

"WOW! I just finished Chuck Togias' hard hitting, in your face book about the state of reality in our country and the world today. Terrorism, Racism, our justice system, and even profiling are some thought provoking topics that will shake the average red-blooded American to the core. This author's quotes and opinions will shock you to think. Such as:

"All suspected terrorists should be profiled, illegally wiretapped, and incarcerated – if our national security is at stake."

"The ACLU is the greatest ally the criminal has EVER had."

"If information gathered through water torture will help

ensure our freedom, I am in complete favor of it."

"These are but a few of the daring sentiments by Mr. Togias, which others are afraid to voice. As a famous actor once said, "The truth – you can't handle the truth." Well, can we? This book will clarify the truth from the lies, that the BS far left spin-doctors mask as political correctness."

— Nick Copanas, Award Winning Sales Executive

"Chuck's book is very intense and he challenges his readers to think about many ideas, two of which are truth and justice. He believes that the current system to enforce the provisions of the fourth amendment must be changed in order to effectively enhance the integrity of the fact finding process. The "rule of reason" is the way to absolute truth, not the illogical suppression or inadmissibility of evidence in court, which will greatly increase the rights of our citizens. I wholeheartedly support his position, and I recommend that you read this book."

— Nichols J. Phillips, retired Actuary and Partner, Pricewaterhouse Coopers

Before We Begin

Author's Introduction to Political Correctness is BS
Since I first wrote my book I have made some minor updates including adding former President Obama's and President Trump's name and making reference regarding our leaving Iraq and Afghanistan. These are minor in scope and did not change the overall theme of my book.

I wrote Political Correctness is BS out of frustration as I indicated in my preface and the events over the last years have only added to my frustration. Benghazi, IRS scandal, Sargent Tahmooressi being held in a Mexican prison, releasing five Muslim terrorists and ISIS are very troubling but unfortunately could have been predicted if we knew how far left and radical President Obama and his administration would be. I feel the "Change" that he and his advisors referred to have blind-sided most responsible Americans!

The main stream media's silence regarding this administration and their irresponsible decisions only add to the insanity.

• **Benghazi** was a disaster and should have been punishable by impeachment yet was virtually over looked by the media and the politically far left of the democratic wing of the party. Our ambassador and four others were murdered in the most horrific way possible and our government never sent troops prior to their eventual execution to help even though they repeatedly cried for help hours before. Can you possibly imagine the reaction of the main stream media if President Bush was in office during this abomination? Anyone that says the Press would not have reacted differently is in complete denial!

- **IRS** scandal where conservatives were being targeted solely because of their politics and the main stream media looked the other way. Ms. Lerner head of the IRS plead the 5th and would not answer questions regarding her role and IRS's role in this illegal practice. Again, I wonder what the main stream media would do if a conservative Republican and their administration were in office and the IRS was targeting liberals?

- **Sgt. Tahmooressi's** incarceration by Mexican authorities who caught him actually trying to turn around and not enter Mexico yet still arrested him. They found three guns in his possession. The Mexican authorities put him in prison on March 31, 2014 and refused to release him. The Obama administration did not, evidently, pressure the Mexicans to let the sergeant go. America had twelve million illegal immigrants in our country draining our economy and this administration was unable to get ONE American back home. Either they were the weakest group ever to occupy the White House or they just didn't care. Whatever the reason it's mind boggling to those with a shred of decency and common sense! I was confident that the sergeant would eventually be released but for him to be incarcerated for more than a day is beyond disgraceful especially in light of our illegal immigration problem from Mexico!

- **Releasing five of the worst terrorists** ever captured by America for an American deserter. Let's see if I got this right. The Obama administration was able to get an American deserter released trading five terrorists who will kill more innocent people yet unable to get Sergeant Tahmooressi, an American who served his country honorably, released from a Mexican prison! This is beyond incompetence and borders on in- sanity. Yet again our main stream media remained silent. It's impossible to discuss this event without wondering if complete lunatics were in charge of our government and as a result the worst was yet to come.

- **ISIS is a complete disaster.** Allowing these murderous fanatics to kill innocence men women and children is criminal and I am usually an isolationist! These monsters are not human and should be destroyed so humanity can survive. Everything they stand for is evil. We must protect those Christians and other non-Muslims from this terror in the name of righteousness! President Obama should have been shouting from the rooftop condemning these fanatics and so should our main stream media! Where were they?

When we look at why Richard Nixon was impeached we must wonder, in comparison, what did he do that was so wrong. Many of us during that period thought that Nixon's removal from office was justified. Comparing his administration with the far-left administration of Obama, I question my prior view. Nixon might have been a thief as many politicians are but I also knew he loved America! I am also convinced that the Obama administration did not!

America has been the beacon to the entire world because of the Core Values upon which it was built. Two of our most important Core Values are our Constitution and our Judeo-Christian belief and principles and both are under attack by the far left seculars and it's destroying the America that we love! America was known as the land of opportunity and people came from all over the world to live their dreams!

My book discusses what the secular far-left's influence is having on America and how it does not reflect or resemble the

America that we once knew! Everything that made America great is being compromised!

We, as Americans, must ask ourselves – "How far will we let this explosion of far left Political Correctness secular insanity assault our government, our lives and our society?"

News flash to our mainstream media: You are supposed to report the news in an unbiased manner not censor it! News censorship is what happens in Communist countries!

Hope you enjoy my book!

CHAPTER 1

America's Deception Media Style

"If you don't read the newspaper, you're uninformed. If you read the newspaper, you're mis-informed."
— Mark Twain.

Collusion-Dems say that Russia interfered with our 2018 election although not one vote, by their own admission, was ever changed. If that is collusion how come the 3 million illegals that illegally voted was not collusion? I wonder if it was not considered collusion because of who they voted for!

1. If socialism is so great why do socialist countries not have an immigration problem? How many people have we seen crossing shark infested waters going from Florida to Cuba? Why did and do so many risk their lives to come here from socialist countries?

2. Obama was a member of the "evil" Reverend Wright's Church for 22 years and his character is never challenged by the main stream media while they are always looking into President Trumps past. Do you think the media may have an agenda regarding Trump? I could not have stayed in Wright's church, if that is what you want to call it, for 22 minutes! Obama did for 22 years and for the media that is not a character issue/problem? I wonder why!

3. The media characterize Trump as anti-Semitic even

though his daughter converted to Judaism marrying her Jewish husband and raising their daughter Jewish. Yet nothing is said regarding Obama and his Muslim upbringing and reverend Wright's anti-Jewish teaching etc., etc., etc.

4. Washington insiders want to see Trump's tax returns and I want to see Obama's college records. What President in the history of our country has ever sealed their college records and WHY? Could it be that he took foreign aid? If not give me one good reason his records are sealed? Unbelievable and the "fair" main stream media do not ever wonder why!

5. Hillary, by her own admission, was dead broke which she announced in the media, started the Clinton Foundation which was supposedly created to help those in need. She worked with Russia on the sale of uranium in which they put millions into her foundation. Yet nothing is said by the media. Hillary now has a net worth of over $150 million and it has never been investigated or been under media scrutiny. Also Benghazi where our ambassador was slaughtered in the most horrific ways possible and the media says nothing even after the Dems tried to blame a movie and its director. Ambassador Stevens called over 600 times for reinforcements and she and her party never responded. I wonder how many times her daughter would have had to call if she was the ambassador? She destroyed over 30,000 emails I wonder why, and still the media is not outraged and looking for answers. What do you think would have happened if Trump was involved and not Hillary, in all of this treachery? The main stream media should hang its head in embarrassment! When will Hillary be investigated by the media? Ha, ha, ha it's my joke for the day!

6. How to achieve a huge majority vote! Why do you think the Dems do not now want a border wall? Do you think it's

because every illegal that enters our country and is allowed to illegally vote will vote for them 100%? Also of all the legal aliens from Mexico that are currently here, that want their families to join them and are obviously pro Mexican will also vote for Dems keeping the Dems in power. It's called block voting. I estimate they could receive from 90-100% of the entire Illegal Mexican and legal Mexican-American vote. Politicians are selling their souls to stay in power. When you are that corrupt how do you sleep at night? As long as the Democrats and their families are not violated by the illegals entering our country they are fine with it and greatly benefit from it!

7. Why are so many Dems throwing their hat in the ring to run for President? Easy answer. When they run for office the money donated to their campaigns that they do not spend they keep. They made the rule. Term limits anyone? That's why the American people should vote for term limits not for the thieves against term limits in Washington! Those that take advantage of this are the greatest con artists ever and they are always pointing to everyone else!

8. I believe Washington has a big problem because it's made up of lawyers and lawyers are process or procedurally focused. They love complexity because the more time it takes to solve a problem the more money they make. Business people, on the other hand, I believe, are outcome focused because the quicker the problem is solved the more money they make. I believe this may be one of the reasons President Trump is having such a tough time being embraced by the political establishment. He is very quick to see and evaluate a problem and then immediately start to solve it. That resonates with me. Example: When I was GSM at an NBC affiliate I was

required to train a team of sales professionals and evaluate their ability to sell advertising and make or exceed their monthly projections. If we did not meet and exceed our projections I would eventually lose my job. Too bad that does not happen in Washington!

9. I propose, in the future whenever there is a Washington shut down no politician gets paid until it's resolved and then I want to see if there will ever be another shut down and if so how long it will last. Many are self-righteous accusers and are always pointing at their rivals while absolving themselves and their party of any wrong doing.

As a leadership consultant I have created five elements to great leadership. I will focus on the first being a Role Model: Great role models will never ask those they lead to do something that they themselves won't do! They will lose all credibility if they do. That's why many of our politicians get little to no respect from the voters. Not all but many are great talkers' bad doers!

10. We as American citizens are always reminded and cautioned by both political parties that Social Security may go broke and I never hear that the politician's retirement plan is ever in trouble. Why? I know I'm being naïve even thinking there is even a chance that they may be working for us and our best interest! Unfortunately many do not!

11. When Judge Kavanagh was being scrutinized by Congress before voting him onto the Supreme Court they went back to his high school days and found that he may have had an illicit affair with a teenage girl in high school which by the way has never been proven. He was seventeen she was fifteen. The far left went insane and wanted him,

immediately, withdrawn. Remember it was High school! I want to first preface my remarks by stating that Kavanagh or anyone else who sexually violates a man, women or child should be prosecuted to the full extent of the law. With no exceptions. The problem I have with their outrage is it's always selective. These selective political condemners rarely if ever investigate themselves or members of their party. They are what I call selective condemners (that's my new term for these Washington phonies)! They are always looking for anything they can blame on others while always absolving themselves and their party from any wrong doing. So I thought of the biblical verse "Those that have not sinned cast the first stone." Do you think that if all those in Congress were investigated from high school till now they might have some serious explaining to do? To me their condemnation is the equivalent of Dracula accusing and condemning the Red Cross for their methods when taking blood. Just imagine if everyone in Congress was investigated from High School till now what would be uncovered? It would be mind boggling I am sure especially in light of their hypocritical condemnation and perceived outrage with Kavanagh! They hate Kavanagh because they are convinced when voting on the Supreme Court he will vote to overturn Roe vs. Wade. See my Chapter entitled: Abortion/Abortionolics!

12. Global warming truth or fiction? There have been many predictions in the past of catastrophic elements created by man that will destroy the world if not addressed. Predictions have been made, in the past that our world will be destroyed due to uncontrolled man made emissions. The question I ask are those making these claims going to benefit from these accusations?

Remember they first called it global warming and when they saw that the earth was not getting warmer, at the rate they predicted, they changed their wording to climate change. Global warming can be disputed climate change cannot. Climate changes four times a year summer, fall, winter and spring. I say follow the money and determine who profits from these accusations. I am always skeptical when Global predictions are made and who profits from these predictions! Follow the money! In fact let's look at 1970 predictions regarding Global Warming. 1. "We are in an environmental crisis which threatens the survival of this nation, and the world as a suitable place of human habitation." Washington University biologist Barry Conner. 2. "Already too late to avoid mass starvation." Dennis Hayes-Chief organizer for earth day. 3. "In a decade urban dwellers will have to wear gas masks to survive air pollution. By 1985 air pollution will have reduced the amount of sunlight reaching earth by one half." Life Magazine. Remember these are 1970 predictions by global experts! That's why I continue to say follow the money and make note of who is profiting!

13. The Wall! Illegal entry into the United States from Mexico is out of control leading to drugs being smuggled into our country and countless deaths of American citizens by Mexican gangs. Yet our "democratic leaders" in Washington are now completely against the wall even though they are on video tape supporting the wall some years earlier. Barack Obama, Chuck Schumer and many other democratic leaders who urged, on video, the building of the wall are now 100% against it. I wonder why? My view of Washington DC and our so called leaders over the years has changed and even more so since Trump has become President. There was a time when

I was young and naive I thought our representatives were for us, the people and now I know that many of them, not all, are for themselves and they profit greatly from the decisions they make. The reason I started to and now like President Trump was when I found out the Washington insiders hated him. The more these Washington insider thieves hate him the more credibility he has with me. The Wall is just an example of the deception and lies they will use to deceive Americans for their own profit. Many have become multi-millionaires while being in office. I wonder how they did it supposedly on a politician's salary. Could the flow of illegal immigrants into our country be making them money? Follow the money!

14. President Trump went to Vietnam to meet with North Korean dictator Kim Jong Un and while he was negotiating the far left democratic socialists within our own country with the help of their counterparts in the media made sure to interrogate former Trump lawyer Michael Cohen, live on Television. I am not sure who chose the date first and could care less but either way I assume the American press knows that for President Trump to be successful in helping the North Korean people and its neighbors live and defeat North Korean oppression America has to look united. So the same day as President Trump is negotiating the Dems and their allies in the main stream media scheduled this atrocity. If the media chose the date first they should still have canceled it out of courtesy and respect for those in harm's way with North Korea. The lives of those affected are too important for the survival of humanity. Like they would have done for any other President. I have no problem with them interviewing Cohen I just have a big problem with the timing of it. The negotiation with North Korea failed! Surprise! Surprise! In any successful

negotiation you have to look united. That's called negotiation 101! I now know without a doubt the radical Dems would rather have President Trump fail/impeached even if it meant his success would improve the lives of humanity than having him succeed and win for America and the world. That is a hatred most responsible people cannot comprehend! Only the radical far left can hate like that! If our country suffered another major depression like in 1929 under President Trump I have no doubt the left would be cheering! They could care less about the average Americans well-being they just want him out. Could this hysteria by the radical socialist far left lead to another civil war in our country? I feel the possibilities are certainly there. There is an old saying and I apply it to the Washington insiders: "Those that cannot do teach." I am not applying this to most teachers just Washington! In the history of America I have never witnessed a situation such as this. I had no idea elements of our population were capable of this!

Two recommendations to help bring America back: First Term limits! I believe that under the current environment we as a nation will continually decline if term limits are not implemented. The problem is the good old boys and girls in Washington will never vote in favor of it. It's like a mafia boss voting to take away his power and go back on the street. The special interest money alone will cost them a fortune. I propose that Americans, as a last resort, start a class action law suit to make term limits happen. Unfortunately our politicians will never have the incentive to change the continued political discourse and do it on their own. It's all about the power and money! Second I want to end this chapter with my grave concerns with our so called unbiased main stream media. They have become anything but unbiased and main stream because of their hatred for President Trump. They are supported by the radical socialist left and have divided our country. If this does not change our country may become so divided against an elected president that our ability to function as a democratic democracy may be in jeopardy and a civil war may be in our future! They are slanting the news and dividing our country and if not corrected we as a nation will lose all credibility here and abroad besides being severely damage as a nation and world power! If not corrected sooner than later we may never recover!

CHAPTER 2

Delusional Deception

"When crime continues to decrease, acceptance will increase."

— C.S. Togias

The continued outrage by the black lives matter group is very puzzling to me. Successful organizations such as large corporations, small and large businesses, sports franchises all the way down to the family all have one thing in common. They have strong leadership and are functional. All of these successful organizations continually build and create strategies to improve their group's performance because effective leadership is judged on their ability to improve the skills and behavior of those they lead. Great leaders are judged on their groups continued improvement and growth and take full responsibility for their successes and failures. They will never blame others for their groups' failures! Their focus is to continually improve never settling for second best. When police enter a high crime area in many inner-city communities they are on edge and rightly so. It's like a soldier entering a combat zone. When a tragic mistake happens and an innocent person who is in the wrong place at the wrong time is violated by police these community leaders will blame everyone but themselves. They rarely if ever blame the criminals who inflict the crime and violence that continually affects so many in their community. If black lives really matter their leaders would come together, create a strategy on how to make these crime ridden communities safe for everyone living in these areas. Instead they point to everyone but themselves and their communities' crime rate soars. Many of these communities are war zones. We should all be judged on our behavior and not color and anyone who judge's solely on color is obviously prejudice and narrow minded! I believe that the overwhelmingly vast majority of Americans judge people on their actions not color! That said these so called inner city community leaders have created this turmoil by not aggressively creating a strategy that would lessen crime in their areas! When crime continues to decrease acceptance will increase! Instead they blame police and white racism for all their communities' misfortune. When there is no crime in a community there is no need for police officers, white or black!

If the black lives matter group is really concerned for black lives why not put all their time, resources and efforts in trying to eliminate crime in their neighborhoods? Because the black lives group has no answers or strategy on how to fix their crime ridden communities they point and blame everyone else. These communities can be fixed. John F. Kennedy said: "every man made problem has a man-made solution." I can't emphasize this enough "great leaders improve the skills and behavior of those they lead." Everything else is secondary. Bad and ineffective leaders point to everyone else. Their communities are in disarray because of their leadership! Period! Black on black crime is out of control and these communities are very dangerous so build a strategy take responsibility and fix the crime problem and stop pointing to everyone else! I want to ask black lives matter and their supporters a question: If America is so bad to Black Americans how come our government gives hundreds of billions of dollars each year to those in need? Many in need are black!

America is the greatest country in the world. People from all over the world come to America for freedom and opportunity. The *political left is always finding fault with America, our Constitution and our Judeo-Christian principles. This has encouraged millionaire athletes to show complete disrespect to our flag and national anthem. Commissioner Roger Goodell and the NFL gave their approval to this complete and utter disrespect.

The late Dr. Stephen Covey who wrote: **7 Habits of Highly Effective People** described how being Principle Centered was virtuous by always judging your thoughts and actions in a morale and ethical way always standing for your beliefs. Covey said the biggest problem for principle centered people will be they may pay a price for standing up for their principles. The commissioner and owners were not strong enough to stand strong for their perceived principles. Who knows if they ever had them but they talk like they did. For these owners to allow these millionaire ungrateful athletes, to disrespect our flag, anthem and country was beyond anything I could have ever imagined! Like the black lives matter group they blame America for their community's crime rate, lack of jobs and school dropout rate. Instead of focusing on the opportunities they were given through college scholarships and multi-million dollar contracts these athletes will only focus on the negative and never blame themselves, their communities' crime rate and lack of family structure. They have been brain washed by finger pointers!

My solution for we Americans who love our country and

condemn this complete disrespect is very easy. You can do one of two things:

1. Do not watch any NFL games including the super Bowl.
2. If you decide to watch the games have a paper and pencil handy and write down each advertiser and do not buy their products!

When you disrespect our anthem you are disrespecting all those who gave their lives to America. The soldiers who died were paid minimum wage to fight and preserve our freedom! These millionaire ungrateful athletes and owners are playing with fire and I am glad they were exposed and revealed to whom they really are!

I thought President Trump bringing up this issue was great because it exposed Goodell and the owners and their lack of character to the American people!

*The far left now refer to themselves as the political left. They must think it makes them seem more in line with American values. Don't be fooled they are the same extreme group that is against prayer in school, unless your Muslim, our Judeo-Christian values and want to change the Constitution and make America a socialist country!

I have written my book to emphasis how the left is trying to change America from a loving Christian democracy to a socialist country with the elimination of our Christian beliefs and the redistribution of wealth. I want to end this chapter with how the main stream media is helping in this effort. I said that if you have a hammer and pound hard enough and long enough you can fit the round peg in the square hole and that is exactly what some in the media do by either spinning the truth or not reporting stories that attack those they agree with to give credence to this socialistic agenda.

When President Trump was still a candidate I could not stand him. I thought he was very arrogant and when as a candidate he spoke during the first debates I would change the station and not listen. Then I started to reevaluate my position when I found out that the Washington insiders hated him. These are many of the same politicians that have become millionaires through their association with special interest groups. I continued to look at him closer when I witnessed the "political left" beating up Trump supporters just for supporting Trump. These were the same type of demonstrators that were spitting on American soldiers when we returned from Vietnam! I concluded that his enemies were my enemies and took a more serious look.

The media and the Washington insiders continually re-enforce my changed position of President Trump by always making a huge issue with everything he does and say almost nothing about his democratic rivals. The Obama administration and democrats could do no wrong with the media. They are always given a pass on their words and actions!

Here are some examples:

• Obama attended Reverend Wright's Church for 22 years. The media made very little of this!

• Obama friendship with anti-establishment and America hating radical Bill Ayers.

• Obama 2008 said "I have campaigned in all 57 states."

• Obama 2012 said: "You have a business. You did not build that business. Someone else did."

• Hillary 1998 said: "Bill is the greatest husband and father

I know. I know no one who is more faithful, true and honest as he is."

• Hillary deleted thousands of confidential emails and has never been prosecuted

• Benghazi when Ambassador Stevens was brutally murdered Hillary said: "What difference does it make." Ambassador Stevens called over 600 times for help prior to no avail.

What would be the reaction with the media if President Trump said or was involved in any of the above? Could he ever have lived it down? These are very few examples there are many, many more!

Hillary is the same person that said she was broke a very few years ago and now is worth over one hundred million dollars. She was heavily involved in the sale of uranium to the Russians which benefited the Clinton Foundation. Hillary is in the pocket of special interest and the media remains silent! On the other hand the media is in frenzy over Mr. Trump winning the 2016 election and Russia's possible involvement. I know one thing he did not sell 20% of America's uranium to Russia and reap millions!

How about someone like democrat Maxine Waters always calling for President Trump's impeachment for not being qualified to serve. She thinks he is stupid and dangerous. This is the same Maxine Waters who was quoted saying: "My fear is if North Korea nukes us, Trump is going to get us into a war." Famous American negotiator Herb Cohen once said there are 3 types of people you cannot negotiate with. Crazy people, stupid people and irrational people! Maxine Waters serves in congress!

Ex NFL quarterback Colin Kaepernick was seen wearing a Fidel Castro T-shirt as a sign of protest to American oppression and many on the left cheered him on. Comparing a tyrant like Fidel Castro to our American government and our way of life is far beyond stupid.

Has Kaepernick done any research on Castro and the number of people his government murdered? If Castro was so great why did so many Cubans risk their lives crossing shark infested waters going from Cuba to Florida? Castro must be a socialist role model for Kaepernick because I am sure he thinks of him as a great leader who was only interested in helping humanity by sharing the wealth with the needy. In reality Fidel Castro was a cold blooded murderer and robbed his people and a testament to that is he was worth over $900 million dollars when he died. I guess he felt that as a socialist leader he did not really have to share his wealth with the common working class! Instead he robbed them. Surprise! Surprise!

America get ready because the left wants to drastically change what made America great. America became the beacon of the world because it offered freedom and opportunity. Because humanity is not perfect America cannot be perfect we are just better than anywhere else in the world. PC is BS!

CHAPTER 3

Political Correctness

Most intelligent conservation experts that have input in helping to preserve our planet on land, sea or air will tell you that exploring under-water is much more difficult and at a much higher risk to our overall environment than exploring on land. Yet on April 20th

2010 British Petroleum (BP) had an oil rig catastrophe in the Gulf of Mexico that may turn out to be the worst marine disaster in the history of mankind. The result is tens of thousands of gallons of oil were gushing into the Gulf daily destroying an unquantifiable number of birds and marine life as well as damaging beaches and waterways. The situation even resolved may be so devastating that the Gulf of Mexico may never fully recovery. The difficulty in trying to stop the leak is magnified because of the deep water BP was drilling in.

If all the experts agree that trying to contain a leak in deep water is so difficult why would BP agree to drill there? It makes no sense to go out so far and so deep if the risks are so enormous. It costs more to drill and from a business stand point makes no sense.

The reason is that many far left activist groups, who are against any drilling, are forcing oil companies away from the shore. These activists groups want clean energy instead of oil but the problem is the world runs on oil. Since clean energy is many years away and they are forcing oil companies to drill off shore the problem is compounded. Many conservationists do not want the drilling close to shore as it might harm the rabbits or some other animal's sanctuary. Instead much more damage will occur to bird and marine life off shore if there is a leak?

These activists have also rejected our exploration of oil in the Rocky mountain region even when the oil reserve is estimated to be larger than that of Saudi Arabia. They do not want us to drill even though the Arabs are in control of the world's oil and they are fleecing America. Besides, as we stated if there was a leak on land it could be controlled in a matter of minutes causing minimal damage to the environment.

It is politically correct to be against oil exploration but is it logical. It is an example of far left activist being able to identify a problem just unable to come up with a logical solution. I am also against off shore drilling because of the danger it poses. I am in favor of drilling in Alaska and the Rockies because we need the oil and Saudi Arabia is not our friend. Since our world runs on oil it may be politically correct to oppose oil exploration but not logical. From an economic point of view it does not make any sense because if we were receiving our oil and gas from the USA, we Americans, would save thousands of dollars due to lower gas prices each year.

America, influenced by a far-left secular, anti-traditional minority is becoming politically correct. Political correctness is affecting our entire thought process. It has prevented most people from expressing their opinions for fear of others labeling them as intolerant. Politically correct activists in our society are little more than special interest groups dedicated to a non-traditional ideology and the majority of them are also very secular in their beliefs. Rejecting anything associated with God!

Many of these activists say they believe in and will defend freedom of speech yet shout down anyone with an opposing point of view. Political correctness amounts to censorship and is promoted and encouraged by those who falsely endorse freedom of speech.

Many far-left activists are attempting to force their secular agenda on the rest of society. They represent gay and lesbian groups that try to gain public acceptance with their efforts to legitimize homosexual marriage even when the majority of Americans oppose it. They are civil rights leaders who are interested in defending the rights of criminals in their communities to the detriment of the victims inside and outside those communities. These leaders change their standard of justice when it is convenient for them to do so. They are school administrators who are more interested in meeting a politically correct curriculum than helping students learn. And of course there are those groups that support the rights of illegal aliens even when it is illegal to do so. Many of these activists are so hysterical in their activism that their message gets lost in the presentation. They use intimidation to achieve their goals.

As a result, most people avoid giving their opinions on anything that may be controversial from fear of others branding them as intolerant. Unfortunately, this has resulted in creating an environment where people have become like sheep remaining silent even when they are in complete disagreement with the vocal minority's ideology. Rather than take a stand and defend their beliefs, most in our society will back off to avoid a conflict. This type of behavior amounts to surrendering values and compromising integrity.

I would like to know what qualifies these activists as the

authority in establishing these politically correct rules. What are their values? Are they morally and ethically sound in their principles? Are these principles leading to our country's revitalization or its devastation? I am totally convinced it is the latter. That is why I wrote Political Correctness is BS—to expose these groups and their false ideology.

My definition of political correctness is simply to create a double standard. That is defined when the rights of one group take precedence over those of another. America is 80% Christian yet the far left are trying to replace our Judeo-Christian values, in favor of their perverted secular value system. This happens when weak indecisive leaders are confronted by aggressive activist groups with a nontraditional agenda. They are given special treatment not afforded to others just to avoid a confrontation.

This, my friend, is not encouraging our freedoms; it is limiting them. It is intimidation and censorship disguised as truth. The more vocal and aggressive the activist groups are the more society conforms to their issues. As I stated earlier far-left politically correct activism is politically correct censorship.

As an example some of the more vocal gay and lesbian groups exemplify this politically correct activism and they will personally attack anyone who does not agree with their lifestyle or agenda. It used to be that if you harassed a homosexual, people considered you homophobic. Now if you simply do not agree with their lifestyle you are homophobic and a bigot. Does this mean that in order not to be homophobic and a bigot you have to agree with the homosexual lifestyle? Why can't those in our society who peacefully disagree with this lifestyle, do so without the threat of intimidation?

For example many Evangelicals believe that homosexuality is a sin. They refer to scripture to defend their position. As long as they do not infringe on the rights of those they disagree with they have every right to express their opinion but are politically incorrect if they do so. In fact it is politically correct and encouraged by the media to attack Evangelicals with this point of view but not politically correct to attack Muslim Fundamentalists who have a much more radical and intolerant view.

Evangelicals disagree with the homosexual lifestyle and pray for their conversion, radical Islam endorse and justify the annihilation of gay and lesbians and are rarely if ever confronted. In fact most far left groups will rarely challenge these Muslim haters but will always confront and attack Evangelicals!

I believe in the sanctity of marriage between a man and a woman but would never want anyone harmed who engages in a gay lifestyle or marriage. I don't know a Christian that would and if I did I would confront them and let them know they would be going against Christ's teachings of tolerance and forgiveness!

Some years ago, I was talking with an actor friend of mine about his profession. He told me many of his fellow actors are homosexual. They sometimes criticize him for being heterosexual. They call heterosexuals breeders. In our politically correct society, would homosexuals who make these comments, be considered heterophobic? Probably not, because there is no heterosexual activist group that would take issue with these comments. In fact heterophobic is so politically incorrect it's not even a word.

In order to gain politically correct status you need to organize an activist group that will vehemently support your far-left issues. If their agenda is attacked, members of this group will do anything to defend their beliefs. To be effective, these groups must have the ability to organize large numbers of people who will aggressively take to the streets in support of their agenda. Their strategy is to intimidate society into accepting their ideology.

Another great example of activist intimidation is the way that illegal immigrants take to the streets in our country and demonstrate their cause. They entered our country illegally then attack those that want our laws obeyed, and, our so called "leaders" fold like lawn chairs. We will cover this in more detail in the immigration chapter of my book.

Non-traditional far left politically correct activist groups are so sensitive that they will react to any comment or situation. In fact, they hope you make a mistake so they can further their agenda. Leaders, and I use that term loosely, like Al Sharpton and Jesse Jackson are a great example of finger pointers always absolving themselves and their communities of responsibility. By the way that's why their communities are well above the national average in crimes committed and never seem to improve. Leaders like these are their community's worst nightmare.

Truth is also not a prerequisite to the far left agenda.

The data supporting their position is not nearly as important as the group interpreting the data. There is an old saying that figures don't lie but liars can figure. That is certainly true in regard to the far-left politically correct and their propaganda.

The media who champion far left causes do not understand

a basic fact: "the messenger can destroy the message" and their declining numbers are a testament. A great example of this is "Mr. McNasty," Keith Olbermann who hates everyone that disagrees with his far left ideology. In fact he dedicated a portion of his, now canceled program, to list the worst people in America. The problem is that he has never included himself on that list. Former far right competitor Glenn Beck I found silly, at times, in his delivery of the message but not hateful.

The far left feel that they have to destroy their detractors and they lose credibility in doing so. Everyone is labeled as "stupid" that does not agree with them. It's my opinion that you have to be stupid to agree with them on most subjects!

To be successful, activist groups feel they must intimidate their opposition. I remember some years ago the book The Bell Curve came out. This book asserted that blacks were not as intelligent as whites or Asians. Was the research true? I have no idea because I never read the book. I do know that the author could have received his information from God and it would not have mattered. Authors Richard J. Herrnstein and Charles Murray were accused of being racist for writing this book. African-American groups demonstrated. Was the research correct? It does not matter, because the content was politically incorrect.

The civil rights activists are aggressive and organized. Many of these black leaders have profited greatly by keeping racism alive. They are waiting for the opportunity to expose a possible racist situation. If that situation does not exist, they can make it appear that it does. That is what activist groups do and they do it well.

I believe that the election of President Obama made many

of the black leaders uncomfortable. They may have to explain how a country they brand as racist could elect a black man as President. But knowing them as I do, they will find other areas of racism to make their point. Con-artists can always con their way out or in!

In contrast, if a book were written stating black athletes are superior to white athletes there would not be any outrage. It is politically correct to discuss white inferiority because whites are the majority and have no white activist groups that would take offense to these comments. Besides, far-left activism has little to do with truth and everything to do with organization and intimidation.

For the record, I am convinced that black athletes are superior to white athletes in most sports. I do not have documented research to back this up. I just have old-fashion research based on sheer numbers. In every sport that attracts black athletes, they have a much higher representation than their percentage of the population. Basketball, football and track and field, are a great example of the success of the black athlete. Black Americans represent only 13% of the population yet 80% of the NBA players, 70% WNBA and 65% of the NFL players are black.

In other words through tremendous effort resulting in outstanding performance by the black athlete they have enhanced and solidified their credibility in the sporting world. You have to earn respect through your efforts not demand it.

Success in sports as well as achieving academic excellence is accomplished by hard work, focus and dedication. I believe most people regardless of race have the capacity to learn. No race is superior in their capacity to learn. Having a desire to learn is another matter.

Some groups stress education more than others. As I have indicated it takes great effort to achieve athletic success and those who put in the effort reap the rewards. It's the same with academic success you reap what you sow and you sow what you reap!

Most white and Asian students who achieve academic success come from an environment that encourages academic achievement. Their families stress education and dedication of purpose. On the other hand, the ghetto culture for the most part, discourages academic effort.

The ability to learn and the desire to learn go hand in hand. As a result, most white and Asian students achieve higher academic scores than their black counterparts. Some black student's who try to focus on academic excellence, are actually harassed by other black students and referred to as Uncle Toms. They are accused of selling out their race.

Can you imagine being part of a culture that thinks learning is a sellout? This is not politically correct to say, but it is a fact. Remember, truth and political correctness, are often diametrically opposed to each other.

In the industrialized cultures education is emphasized and encouraged. In the Third-World culture, it is not. That is why they remain Third World. What type of leadership could ever endorse this Third World mentality? Ineffective leaders, such as Al Sharpton and Jesse Jackson never have to take responsibility for the lack of achievement of those they are influencing and leading. It is too easy to blame others for their lack of success and, unfortunately, it is politically correct to do so. They have to blame America's racism for their lack of community success. You will never, ever hear them place blame on themselves. That is what bad leaders and far left activists do they always blame others for their failures and unfortunately it has been very lucrative for them to continue doing so while destroying their communities.

Many black leaders still blame racism for the inner city students' low academic achievement. That, in my opinion is shifting the blame and a complete cop-out. Creating an environment to learn should be the community leaders' and parents' top priority and responsibility.

There is a lot of violence in ghetto schools. These schools are disruptive and not conducive to learning, yet they are never the issue with the far left PC gang. It is easier to blame racism on a failed school district and the lack of qualified teachers willing to teach in these schools than to hold students responsible for the classroom violence and their unwillingness to learn.

Why would good teachers ever want to teach in an unsafe school where they would be harassed and ridiculed for their efforts? When you do not identify and correct problems, it will lead to problems that are more serious. As a result, the politically correct are criticizing our education system for its racist inadequacies instead of focusing on the real problem— the students' lack of desire and effort to learn because of their lack of community and parental leadership.

When you refuse to take personal responsibility for your actions it will usually result in personal failure. Example: it is impossible to become a good athlete without practicing long hours and it's as difficult to excel in the classroom without studying. It's again a "reap what you sow..." analogy.

It has become more important to teach students with politically correct guidelines than it is for students to become educated. Those guidelines include not confronting unruly student behavior and implementing an inadequate curriculum designed to appease the politically correct school boards.

In Thomas Sowell's wonderful book Black Rednecks and White Liberals, the author gives many examples of how not following a politically correct agenda has helped students learn. Sowell writes:

The principal of Bennett Kew School in Englewood, California, whose student body is 52% Hispanic and 45% Black, raised these children's reading levels from the third percentile to the fiftieth percentile in just four years. However, she was threatened with loss of money because she used phonics instead of the mandated "whole language" teaching methods and taught exclusively in English, instead of using the "bilingual" approach required by education authorities. The fact that she was succeeding where they were failing carried no weight with state education officials. Fortunately, it carried enough weight with the parents of her students that they bombarded these officials with protests that caused them to relent and let this principal continue to succeed in her own way, instead of failing in their way.

Just think the politically correct school board was going to disband a successful curriculum because it did not fit the guidelines of the politically correct board of education. It makes you wonder if they were interested in teaching children or simply wanted to score politically correct points to meet a misguided agenda. Unfortunately, for the students, I think we know it is the latter.

As I've said in my previous book, **Create Loyal Customers in an Unloyal World**, great leaders should be judged by their ability to improve the skills and behavior of those they lead. Everything else is secondary. There is great potential in the black community and it will only be maximized when they have real leaders not finger pointers!

Let me give you yet another example of this misguided politically correct ideology. An art museum displayed a painting of a man flushing the **Holy Bible** down the toilet. Many who viewed the painting were outraged. The museum's director, when confronted, defended the artist's right to display his artwork and would not remove it. By his standards, it was a matter of free speech.

When the director was asked if he would display the same artwork with the Koran being flushed down the toilet he emphatically replied no. The desecration of the Bible was politically correct to the director so it was a freedom-of-speech issue, but the desecration of the Koran was politically incorrect, and therefore not a freedom-of-speech issue. The art director never let logic or truth affect his thinking.

This is why the far-left politically correct distorted agenda and those who endorse it have no credibility. Those who establish the criteria are themselves biased. Political correctness is based solely on a double standard and is therefore unfair. I cannot emphasize this enough.

Political correctness has reached an all time absurdity with the proposed building of the Muslim Mosque near the site of ground zero. Either former president Obama, who supported the building of the mosque, is not as intelligent as we once thought or he was delusional if he did not understand the message that the lunatics in Islam were trying to convey. The Muslim Fundamentalist must be shaking their heads in disbelief that it was even being considered. Political correctness, if approved, would have allowed Islam to build a symbol to celebrate their devious acts of terror and anyone that thinks otherwise is not thinking! It's again an example of far left idealism versus realism. In other words BS vs. Truth!

What is even more ridiculous is Islam trying to con Americans into feeling guilty for opposing the building of the mosque and unbelievably many on the far left were falling for the con. Saudi Arabia who is a major proponent of this mosque has no churches or synagogues and does not allow Christians or Jews to practice their religion.

There are over 1200 mosques in the USA and 100 in New York City. Yet these Muslim hypocrites, who deny religious rights in their own country, are passing judgment on America.

If America is intolerant how should we characterize Islam and its hateful, murderous doctrine? If Islam's intentions were honorable why didn't they organize huge rallies in New York City after 9/11 denouncing terrorism? The reason for building this mosque was a complete con game perpetuated by liars and con artists and many on the far left are so misguided that they have become part of the con.

These are the same secular far left politically correct activists that removed prayer from public schools and all reference to God from public buildings. Even though 80% of America is Christian. Is their religious tolerance only for those without tolerance?

It again demonstrates a complete distorted double standard by the far left political correct elite. Are they that misguided and ignorant or do they hate our Judeo-Christian values, upon which our country was built, that much that they will resort to anything to change America?

The following chart demonstrates the difference in being politically correct vs. being politically incorrect.

POLITICALLY CORRECT	POLITICALLY INCORRECT
Miss Black America Contest	Miss White America Contest
Building a Mosque on Ground Zero	Opposing the Mosque on Ground Zero
Far left secular ideology removing anything related to God from public buildings	Public display of the 10 Commandments or reference to God in public buildings
Defending the rights of illegal immigrants	Enforcing our laws in regard to illegal immigration
Gay & Lesbian Parade	Heterosexual Parade
All-Black Colleges	All-White Colleges
Holiday Greeting	Christmas Greeting
Atheist Rights	Praying in School
Jewish & Arab Religious Symbols during Christmas	Displaying a Manger in Public

This indicates an absolute double standard and makes sense only to those who have a distorted self serving politically correct agenda. The far lefts distortion of the truth makes it impossible to achieve a fair and logical solution.

Note: The far left political correct always talk about their love for humanity: Have you ever seen a far left mass demonstration that was peaceful? Every mass far left demonstration that I ever witnessed cars are overturned, stores are robbed, people are beating up, police are stoned and this is all done in the name of humanity!!

CHAPTER 4

The Injustice System

"When injustice becomes law resistance becomes duty"
— Thomas Jefferson.

Attorneys are always trying to alert the public regarding products and services that have been misrepresented by the manufacturer and caused harm or death to the unsuspecting public. These suits are known as class action law suits. Class action law suits are the equivalent of winning the lottery for the attorneys who represent the victims. Most litigants in these law suits get pennies on the dollar while their attorney's make millions.

If you read my previous book **Mouth Off**, you know that I have great concerns with our judicial system. Lawyers run it for the benefit of lawyers. It is a procedural system and often has little to do with logic or truth (to further my point I will include 7 verdicts at the end of this chapter that may astound you).

Many times through procedural technicalities, violent criminals are put back on the street to violate additional innocent people. When states have tried to impose mandatory sentencing for crimes against children, the criminal defense attorneys and judges are their biggest opposition. It takes away their power. They do not take into consideration how it affects society, because they are process focused not outcome focused.

Criminal defense attorneys always talk about the rights of the accused and say that everyone is entitled to a fair trial. Yet they purposely try to keep damaging evidence, which indicates their clients' guilt, from the jury. Even when they know that the evidence is undeniably true. Is that justice or is that helping their clients escape punishment for their crimes? They do not want justice; they want injustice in favor of their clients. Many are wolves in sheep's clothing. **The justice system encourages and justifies injustice.**

When this happens, it is a sham disguised as truth perpetuated by those whose job it is to distort the truth. Outcomes, such as the O.J. fiasco, are the rule not the exception. Especially for those who can afford to hire veteran lawyers who will manipulate the system. Our system is not a black and white system; it is a rich and poor system. The richest in our society benefit from this injustice.

The system also benefits those who support a far-left agenda. The civil rights of America's enemies are being defended by the far-left ACLU to meet their nontraditional ideology as we previously discussed. In fact, they will defend any activist group, including potential terrorists or Muslim fundamentalist sympathizers. The crazier the cause the more involved the ACLU will become.

An example of this happened when six Muslim clerics were removed from a US Airways flight because of what passengers thought was strange, aggressive behavior. In light of 9/11, the passengers were very uncomfortable with the clerics and reported them to the airline authorities. The clerics were removed and the flight continued. End of story, right? Wrong. The clerics and their lawyers sued US Airways and the passengers for their removal. This is nonsense. After

9/11, any passenger who would not alert authorities to any suspicious behavior, especially by Muslim clerics, would have to be insane.

The clerics are angry because they feel authorities profiled them for being Muslims and, therefore, discriminated against them. Are they kidding? They know that airports are on very high alert to any suspicious behavior, so what do they do? They chant, pray, and make disparaging remarks loudly enough for the passengers to hear. What a setup. They are using our judicial system against us and the system encourages it. If this lawsuit goes through—and I am sure it did—then there is no one regardless of the situation free from lawsuits. A lawyer's dream, come true.

Two things would have happened if they'd won the lawsuit and they are both bad for society. First, there would be thousands of similar suits filed if there is any hint of profiling. Second, it would make authorities hesitate to ever confront anyone they suspect is a terrorist threat. The first scenario helps lawyers and the second helps terrorists. Both are bad for innocent airline passengers. If they would have succeeded with the suit, gas up and drive to your next destination.

The cleric incident falls under what is known as having "probable cause." "Probable cause" is one of these areas that is very difficult to understand and many times escapes logic. Let me give you another example. If a police officer searches an automobile, finds a dead body in the trunk, but did not have probable cause for that search—the discovery of the body could be inadmissible at trial. In other words, the driver of the car will not have to account for the body discovered in the trunk. This logic sounds insane to logical, nonjudicial people and yet, it happens every day when police do their jobs and have their efforts negated by judicial procedures.

Let me give you another example of how corrupt and unfair our judicial system can be. In our nation's capital Washington, DC, a laundry owner lost a customer's pair of trousers. When this happens, it can be very inconvenient for the customer but not the end of the world. I mean, there is hunger and despair around the world, so we should all be able to take in stride a lost pair of trousers, right? Apparently not.

The customer was so outraged, that he sued the laundry owner for $54 million. This is not a joke and the insanity does not stop there. The customer was no ordinary customer—he was a judge. That's right a judge sued a small-business owner for $54 million for losing his trousers. A judge who presides over court cases and supposedly renders impartial verdicts was the litigant in this horrendous lawsuit. The laundry owner, trying to avoid prosecution offered a $12,000 settlement through his lawyer for a pair of trousers. I am not making this up; he had to hire a lawyer (the judicial system wins again) for this nonsense. The "honorable" judge refused the $12,000 settlement and proceeded with the suit. He refused a $12,000 settlement for a pair of trousers. They must have been really nice trousers.

I am thrilled this happened because it demonstrates how corrupt and manipulative the system can be. Judges understand, more than any of us, how to work the system with its many procedures. Do you think it may be time for court reform? The judicial system has become a joke and the joke is on the rest of society. It is manipulating the society that the system is supposed to be serving.

If the judicial system were legitimate, this judge would be

disbarred and be liable for the mental anguish he caused this small-business owner. Knowing this situation, would anyone feel comfortable with this judge rendering any decision for them or their family? This case and this judge in particular should be a complete embarrassment to the entire judicial system. I wonder how many judges and lawyers came to the defense of this judge and condone his actions. I am sure there were some.

The "honorable" judge Roy Pearson lost his law suit when presiding judge, Judith Bartnoff determined that "a reasonable customer would not interpret 'satisfaction guaranteed' to mean that a merchant is required to satisfy a customer's unreasonable demands that the merchant has reasonable grounds to dispute."

I am glad the defendant won but how any court could even hear this nonsense is unbelievable. The defendant Soo and Jin Chung of Custom Dry Cleaners case was dismissed. I just wonder how much it cost them in legal fees.

I once asked a judge to give me his opinion on a hypothetical situation. A suspected criminal was charged with murder. In fact, authorities found a video of him shooting another man in the head. The judge, defense attorney, and prosecutor all viewed the videotape. The problem was that the tape was secured without following proper procedures and was therefore inadmissible at trial. With no other evidence, the criminal, was set free. I asked the judge "is that justice?" Without hesitation, he replied yes. He went on to say, this is the way our system works. If this type of injustice is the way our system works, that means that the system is broken. It is not fair, logical, or moral to the rest of society and yet very acceptable to the judicial community. I wonder if judges would feel this way if one of their family members were the victim.

When I closely evaluate our judicial system, I realize that procedures have precedence over truth. Remember, inadmissible evidence does not mean that the evidence is wrong. It just means that the process used to gather the evidence was not followed correctly. The justice system is out of control because procedures rule the system. Who do these procedures benefit, the innocent or the guilty?

When criminal defense attorneys use these procedures to keep truthful incriminating evidence from the jury and the guilty go free, how can anyone call this justice? When I continually hear criminal defense attorneys justify their tactics, I can see why many of us think they are worse than the criminals they defend. Everything in our world that is legitimate must be based on truth. Yet, our judicial system, which is based on procedures, has become devoid of truth through its legal manipulative tactics.

This type of justice has to change because it is injustice and I have a couple of ideas. The first thing I think we should do is to look for qualified political candidates that are not lawyers. Our judicial system affects our political system and vice versa. Congress makes the laws and the judicial system interprets the laws. Lawyers are in both houses of Congress and have great impact on the laws of our country. We need to change the political mix because lawyers love complexity and tend to be much more interested in the process than in the solution. Remember the more confusing the process the more money they make.

As I stated in chapter one business executives are outcome

focused lawyers are processed focused. Procedures create loopholes and loopholes benefit the criminal defense attorney while adversely affecting society. Truth is in the verdict, which is easily manipulated. The verdict may actually exacerbate the problem because it sets a precedent.

That is why politicians have such a hard time making decisions. Most politicians are lawyers and lawyers love complexity and ambiguity. We must give others in our society besides lawyers (ex. Trump), with common sense, a chance to influence the system. They would bring clarity and a logical viewpoint to the process because their focus would be on a logical outcome instead of applying a smoke and mirror mentality that benefits only them. Everyone but lawyers understands that when the process prevents a logical outcome you change the process instead of defending it.

It is human nature for any group to try to benefit themselves. I have always said that if we had a majority of politicians who were cab drivers making the laws in Washington, then we would all be required to take a cab to work. Various professions bring various kinds of expertise and will help bring a commonsense approach to our process-rigged judicial and political systems.

If we had others besides lawyers regulating the effectiveness of the judicial system we could then review all of the current procedures and evaluate their effectiveness. Especially those designed to keep incriminating evidence from the jury. Our system should encourage and guarantee that all truthful information be accessible to the judge and jury to ensure a fair verdict. Lawyers on their own will never do this because it brings clarity and their income derives from confusion. We should eliminate any procedure designed to prevent the truth from being revealed. Justice should be synonymous with truth.

We could then form watchdog committees and keep a record of criminals avoiding jail time through technicalities. Review all elements in the procedural system that allows technicalities to exist and help to legislate, a change in these procedures.

To force this legislation we could keep track of all criminals released through judicial manipulation and review their post-release histories. How many thousands of violations did they commit? I'm sure the numbers would be staggering. When these violations are documented and publicized, the public can see firsthand the risk these criminals pose and more importantly how the system is failing. Once revealed the public outcry will force legislation to rectify the situation. The judicial system will no longer be able to justify these procedural loopholes.

A friend of mine sent me this email regarding some outrageous verdicts rendered. These verdicts will speak for themselves. You judge and see if we need to revamp the system.

#1: A women in Texas was awarded $80,000 by a jury after breaking her ankle tripping over a toddler who was running inside a furniture store. The store owners were understandably surprised by the verdict considering the running toddler was her own son.

#2: A man in Los Angeles won $74,000 plus medical expenses when his neighbor ran over his hand with their Honda Accord. Apparently the victim didn't notice there was someone at the wheel of their car when he was attempting to steal their hub caps.

#3: A Pennsylvania man was leaving a house he had just burglarized by way of the garage. Unfortunately for him the automatic garage door opener malfunctioned and he could not get the garage door open. Worse he couldn't re-enter the house because the door connecting the garage locked when he pulled it shut. He was forced to sit for 8 days and survive on a case of Pepsi and a bag of dry dog food. He sued the home owner's insurance company claiming undue mental anguish. The jury said the insurance company must pay $500,000 for his anguish. Remember he was burglarizing the house!

#4: An Arkansas man was awarded $14,500 and medical expenses after being bitten on the butt by his neighbor's dog even though the dog was on a chain in his owner's yard. The man did not get as much as he asked for because the jury believed the dog might have been provoked because the man climbed over the fence into the yard and repeatedly shot the dog with a pellet gun.

#5: A Pennsylvania women was awarded $113,000 after she slipped on a spilled soft drink at a Philadelphia restaurant and broke her tail bone. The reason the soft drink was on the floor was that she had thrown it at her boyfriend 30 seconds earlier during an argument.

#6: A lady in Delaware sued the owner of a night club in a near by city because she fell from the bathroom window to the floor, knocking out her 2 front teeth. The women, was trying to sneak through the ladies room to avoid paying a $3.50 cover charge. The woman was awarded $12,000 plus dental expenses.

#7: I am saving the most out outrageous for last. In Oklahoma a women who purchased a 32 foot Winnebago motor home was suing for damages. On her first trip home from an Oklahoma University football game having driven onto the freeway she set the cruise control at 70 miles an hour and calmly left the drivers seat to go to the back of the Winnebago to make herself a sandwich. Not surprisingly the motor home left the freeway crashed and overturned. She sued Winnebago for not putting in the owners manual that she couldn't actually leave the drivers seat while the cruise control was set. Get ready for this: the Oklahoma jury awarded her $1,750,000 plus a new motor home. Winnebago has actually changed the manual due to the suit.

Wasn't former Vice Presidential Candidate John Edwards a personal injury attorney?

If we wait for lawyers to make the system fair and streets safe by changing their system, we will be waiting forever. The lawyers will always justify the system. Ambiguity provides them a great living at society's expense.

CHAPTER 5

Terrorism

The dictionary describes the meaning of terrorism as the systematic use of terror as a means of coercion. Couple terrorism with religious fanaticism and you've described the Muslim fundamentalist. They are out-ofcontrol religious zealots dedicated to the destruction of humanity. They are inhumane monsters who will even kill women and children in the name of their God.

The opinions I express in this chapter do not in any way reflect on the average law-abiding Arab's in our country or around the world. Arabs are not the problem. I have many Syrian Christian friends who are wonderful people and great Americans. That said it is my opinion that the Muslim fundamentalist, not Arabs, are the most dangerous threat to humanity the world has ever known. That includes the Nazis before and during WWII.

The reason is that there are 1.2 billion Muslims around the world, that's 22% of the world's population and many of them have such a distorted view of right and wrong. They refer to non-Muslims as subhuman yet tie explosives to their own children to be martyrs. Their thought process is contrary to anything that our civilized society has been subjected to. They kill innocent men, women, and children in the name of Allah. If Allah tells them to tie explosives around their children to gain immortality, then what worse could the devil tell them to do?

The moderates within their religion are afraid to speak out against this barbaric behavior for fear of death, which compounds the problem. Their views of right and wrong are impossible for honest, moral men and women to comprehend. When being confronted with this savage enemy we are trying to be conventional. In the United States, our judicial system is being used against us. We are scrutinized for our interrogation methods by the far left in our own country. The PC protected, criticize our government for being too harsh when dealing with these terrorists. In the meantime, when Muslim fundamentalists capture a Christian or Jew, they cut off their heads.

The Muslim fundamentalists are at war with us and we are at war with each other. Of the 1.2 billion there are supposedly only 10 million hard core Muslim fundamentalists. This number is in question because so many so-called moderates preach a similar hateful message. This was verified when the British government placed a hidden camera in a so-called, moderate established mosque in England. They openly discuss their hatred for the West and everything we stand for. They will not rest until they dominate or annihilate all of us and are very committed to this end. Yet as a country, I do not think the majority of our citizens take this threat seriously. I know that the far-left politically correct think this terrorist issue is a non-issue and will go away when we leave Iraq and Afghanistan.

I agree that our country's decision to invade and occupy Iraq without a clear exit strategy was a big mistake. It has divided our country. I think many Americans feel that we have brought this Muslim terrorist problem upon ourselves, and that is where I disagree. These crazy Muslim fundamentalist have used Iraq and Afghanistan as an excuse to organize the religious fanatics within their culture who are dedicated to annihilating all non-Muslims. I knew that when we left both countries we would still have this Muslim fundamentalist problem. Crazy fanaticism is rarely appeased because lunatics are lunatics. By the way we have left these countries and terrorism got much worse globally until President Trump took over.

Our intentions in invading Iraq were to overthrow an evil dictator who had an arsenal of nuclear weapons, and bring democracy to the region. Neither, was accomplished because Saddam did not have the weapons and democracy could not bring peace. I do not know why we feel that we have to bring democracy to the entire world anyway. We were occupying 2 countries where they not only hate us they hate each other. They send suicide fanatics to kill Americans and each other.

I feel democracy cannot work in most Arab countries where Muslim fundamentalist have an influence. These fundamentalists will not tolerate political dissent or allow freedom of speech, and both are essential to a democracy. Occupying these countries had to be one of the most miscalculated military strategies, ever! Our government officials did not do their homework in analyzing the culture of the Iraqi and Afghan people prior to our invasion. If they had, we would not have occupied these countries.

We should have learned our lesson in Vietnam. We tried to install a democracy there and were defeated. The culture was not conducive to a democracy. Being a Vietnam veteran and seeing firsthand how futile our efforts were in trying to create a democracy there, I became an isolationist. I feel it is a waste of American lives to liberate countries just for the sake of imposing our democratic beliefs. Besides, isn't it the UN's responsibility to bring peace to embattled countries? If not, what is the UN's purpose?

This said, we must remember that these crazy terrorists bombed the World Trade Center before we invaded Iraq. They are only using our occupation of Iraq and Afghanistan as an excuse to commit more acts of terrorism. There are some crazy, misguided far left people in this country, who think our government brought down the World Trade Center. However, the rest of us normal, logical people remember that it was the Muslim fundamentalists (Al-Qaeda) that caused 9/11. They also committed many more acts of aggression prior to 9/11. Here are just a few examples:

- 1968: Senator Bobby Kennedy was assassinated by a male Muslim extremist
- 1972: Munich Olympics, Jewish athletes were murdered by Muslim extremists
- 1979: US Embassy in Iran was taken over by Muslim extremists holding Americans hostage
- October 23, 1983: Marine barracks in Beirut, Lebanon, were destroyed by a Muslim suicide bomber, killing 220 marines
- 1988: Pan Am Flight 103 was bombed by Muslim extremists
- February 26, 1993: car bombing of the World Trade Center, which killed six people and caused $300 million in damage was the act of Muslim extremists
- 1998: US Embassies in Kenya and Tanzania were bombed by Muslim extremists

• October 12, 2000: the USS Cole, under the command of Kirk Lippold, was attacked; seventeen sailors were killed and thirty-nine injured by Muslim extremists

More recently in Fort Hood, Texas we had an American Muslim Army psychiatrist Major Nidal Malik Hasan kill 13 soldiers and wound 38. Major Nadal was not only an American soldier he was a psychiatrist supposedly qualified and dedicated to helping soldiers with mental problems. They say he was inspired by a Muslim religious leader. In normal religions when you are inspired by your religious leaders it is for good and humane reasons.

Major Nidal is a home grown terrorist that demonstrated, prior to the shootings, strange, aggressive behavior and was not investigated. It was not politically correct to investigate or remove Major Nidal because it would have been profiling him as a Muslim. Instead 13 American soldiers are dead. When will we ever learn?

Does this sound like a pattern and should we be concerned with Muslim fundamentalists? Would we be justified in profiling Muslims in our airports to ensure the safety of our citizens? Especially since all of these attacks were prior to our occupation of Iraq (except Major Nadal). They deliberately attack our citizens and troops and continue to do so. These attacks were unprovoked and there are many more examples. I have listed only a few. Be assured of one thing— whether we are in Iraq, Afghanistan or not, the Muslim fundamentalists are dedicated to our complete demise. This is a religious war being waged by religious lunatics. It is not about occupied land, be assured of that.

Also, be assured that the war on terror is real whether we

believe it or not. These fanatics will use all methods necessary to complete their diabolic mission to rid the world of everyone who is not a Muslim. In my opinion, it is not *whether* there is going to be another 9/11—but *when*.

These are religious fanatics who will hide among women and children and fire their weapons at our soldiers. They hide in their mosques and conduct open warfare against us. When we return fire, they accuse us of killing their women and children and destroying their mosques. They distort and oppose everything we know to be truth and justice, because of their twisted ideology. They are impossible to negotiate with. Their fanaticism justifies lying and the killing of all non Muslims. Just think of what this world would be like if they were in control of humanity.

We have this type of enemy waging war against us and we are worried about profiling. I want all suspected terrorists to be profiled. In fact, I want them to be illegally wiretapped and incarcerated, if, we feel our national security is at stake. We are worried about their civil rights and they are dedicated to annihilating us.

It is politically correct nonsense perpetrated by the PC protected in our society. Those who criticize but never physically engage in battle will always verbally attack those who do their fighting. It is so easy to be an enlightened idealist when everyone else does your fighting for you.

Does Guantanamo Bay prison bother me? Not in the least. Also I am completely against civil trials for captured terrorists. They will use our flawed judicial system to further their cause.

Our government makes many mistakes and is far from perfect. Our occupation of Iraq was an example of a misguided strategy. Our government, with all its flaws, is not barbaric and never participates in acts of terrorism against innocent people.

We as a people along with our government try hard to do what is right regardless of what the far left claim. The mistakes we make are unfortunately, motivated by greed. The division and undermining between our two political parties is for power and money. We are not always a great example for the world to see, but in comparison to these crazy Muslim fundamentalists and their inhumane brutality, we are a shining light.

Our goals are to seek equality for all, women's rights, and religious tolerance. We do not beat women in the square because their wrists are uncovered. We do not kill homosexuals and we do allow Muslims in our country to pray as they choose without the fear of death. The politically correct with their secular views should be most concerned with these Muslim fanatics. Many of the far left politically correct follow a secular doctrine, devoid of religious beliefs, which would not be tolerated, by these intolerant religious lunatics.

I have heard some people in the entertainment field compare the religious right with the Muslim fundamentalist. Anyone making this ridiculous comparison is delusional. I will agree with the comparison as soon as Christian mothers tie explosives to their children and send them out as martyrs. That will never happen in a civilized Christian or Jewish society. This can only happen in a deranged culture where human life is considered worthless. Any person comparing the religious right in the United States with Muslim fundamentalists does not have the slightest idea of how dangerous these fundamentalist are.

Here are two examples I found when researching Shariah Law: Let's compare the Muslim Fundamentalist religion to the religious right in our country and see if there is a comparison: Afghanistan: Strict interpretation of Islamic law calls for the death penalty for any woman found in the company of a man other than a close family member. Sexual activity is assumed to have happened. A women Jamila, was found guilty of trying to leave the country with such a man. She was caught and stoned to death on March 28, 1996.

The second example is again Afghanistan: Under the previous, Taliban, regime, a woman, Nurbibi, 40, and a man Turylai, 38, were stoned to death in a public assembly using palm size stones. They were found guilty of non-martial sex. Turylai was dead within 10 minutes, but Nurbibi had to be finished off by dropping a large stone on her head.

Mr. Wali, head of the Office for the Propagation of Virtue and the Prohibition of Vice, expressed satisfaction with the execution: "I am very happy because, it means that the rule of Islam is being implemented." These executions, as well as hand amputations for convicted thieves, are regarded as religious occasions and are not viewed by non-Muslims.

It would be impossible for anyone that is seeking the truth to compare Christianity with this barbaric behavior. There has never been a Christian group that would condone this treachery, ever! These actions are beyond horrific.

The former prime minister of Israel, Golda Meier, was once asked if there would ever be peace, in the Middle East. She replied, "There will only be peace when the Arab mothers love their children more than they hate the Jews." Normal societies cannot comprehend that kind of hate. All Americans better wake up and understand the enemy we face.

These Muslim fundamentalist are the most dangerous people the world has ever encountered. Their thought process is so distorted that they are impossible to reason or negotiate with and we have those on the far left minimizing their threat. I once heard someone say that not all Muslims are terrorists but all terrorists are Muslim. Not all terrorists are Muslims but the Muslim Terrorists are the only ones that sacrifice their children, in the name of God and are dedicated to killing everyone who is not Muslim. That type of insanity is unprecedented. Unfortunately, that statement is true.

I hope and pray that the moderate Muslims will have the courage to take back their religion before it is too late.

The thing that bothers me the most about the American Muslims is their silence on this issue. You never see or hear of them conducting huge rallies in support of America. There is no flag waving or shouts of loyalty to America. They are so silent on the issue it makes you wonder where their loyalties really lie. They should love us or leave us because they know more than anyone about the evil doctrine of the Islamic fundamentalists. The only conclusion I can come to is that they are either afraid to speak out or they are in agreement with the terrorists. I hope and pray it is not the latter.

Americans must come together as a nation and recognize how serious the Islamic terrorist threat is. We will make a conscious effort to solve this problem only when we understand the seriousness of the problem and what concerns me is I am not convinced that President Obama did understand the seriousness of the problem. When as President Obama stated that Palestine and Israel will be treated the same, that, in my opinion, was a big mistake because one is a trusted ally and Palestine is Muslim and therefore a questionable supporter at best.

If America looks weak on this issue it will embolden our enemy. There is an old army quote: "an army of lions led by a lamb will be defeated by an army of lambs led by a lion." I was hoping that our former Commander and Chief President Obama was not a lamb. I was wrong.

We have two choices to confront this evil now or suffer the consequences later. We need to let the Muslim fanatics, know that they will be aggressively challenged whenever they try to impose their deranged ideology through terrorist tactics on the rest of the world. They must see America, strong and united, ready to combat tyranny whenever challenged.

We must close our borders, north and south, immediately. No one should ever again be able to enter into our country without a background check and proper documentation. Open borders make easy access for the terrorist element to enter our country undetected. These people want to hurt us and we should not make it easy for them to do so.

We should identify and register all known suspected terrorists similar to the way we register sex offenders. Once registered, we should consistently monitor their movements and share this information with law enforcement agencies around the country, put them in prison or deport them.

We should randomly monitor mosques in the United States with surveillance techniques to uncover hate speech designed to create homegrown, terrorists. We should have learned our lesson with Major Nadal. This is a Fourth Amendment issue and we should suspend the Fourth Amendment for known or suspected terrorists at this time. Let us not let the politically correct in our judicial system continue to be our demise.

We must continue to pledge our support for Israel.

The terrorists must understand that a nuclear attack on Israel would be considered an attack on the United States. Israel is our friend and ally and we must never forsake them. We share the same traditional values and we believe in life, liberty, and the pursuit of happiness for all. Both of our countries allow political dissent and we do not kill those who disagree with our religious beliefs. In other words, we have much in common, because we are civilized.

We are engaged in a war with a very vicious enemy and if we play by our judicial rules, they will win. We must level the playing field and not let the politically correct protected ACLU help defeat us. We should never allow our judicial system to permit and encourage Muslim Fundamentalists to advance their distorted religious ideology against U.S. citizens. When the laws of our country are defending the criminals' rights and not protecting its citizens we are all at risk.

When researching the terrorist's mentality I thought it would be impossible to successfully reason with this type of distorted mindset and I was frustrated as you can sense in this chapter. After reflecting on what I had written I did not want to end this chapter without having some type of positive solution to this seemingly impossible situation. Then I thought, as I often do, of a famous John F. Kennedy quote: "Every man-made problem has a man-made solution" and tried to devise a well thought-out simple plan that would end this senseless global slaughter. I wanted to use logic rather than to continue to endorse more military aggression to counter act terrorism. This is simple logic that would even register to the most religious terrorist.

The problem: How to counter-act terrorism using our industrial technology not military aggression?

Our current military strategy has only created martyrs and increased the terrorist's resistance as well as taken the lives of many American soldiers. Instead of helping to alleviate the problem we've compounded it.

My simple idea: **We should create a technology that would coat all of our weapons with pork residue. Every bullet, bomb, piece of scrap metal, every weapon that we take into combat should be coated. All weapons!**

Then we would announce that we want peace throughout the world and we will leave all Muslim countries to let them settle their differences among themselves making them aware of our new weapon technology. These Muslim terrorists will never stop killing innocent men, women and children because they think "their God" instructs them to do so no matter what we say or do using conventional wisdom. They also believe that contact with pork upon death prevents them from going to "their heaven." To argue with this type of insanity is impossible so let them understand the consequences of their actions by talking to them, not arguing, using their frame of reference. Do not threaten them, let them perceive their outcome, if their aggression continues with America and let them decide! We would also give this new weapon technology to Israel and to our police departments in the USA!

The following is my three step patent on how to eliminate world terrorism.

1. To combat world terrorism all manufactured weapons in America, from this day forward, will be coated in pork residue. All weapons!

2. Our military will create a video that will describe the entire process from the development of the pig residue to the actual coating of the weapon. This will make it perfectly clear to friend and foe that we have the technology and have implemented it.

3. We will have our field commanders meet with our allies to make them fully aware of our new technology. They will present our strategy in a way that will encourage the world leaders to understand that we are striving for a peaceful resolution that will save lives.

No logical peace loving person could be against my strategy because it will prevent the needless loss of lives on both sides caused by Muslim extremists while saving billions of dollars that are now spent to fight terrorism.

I have applied for a patent for the above idea! My patent will only be effective if all weapons used in combat from this day forward are coated with pork! ALL WEAPONS forever coated!

I am adding this quick note to end my chapter on Terrorism since the Obama administration signed a nuclear arms deal with Iran. I am trying to figure out if Obama and his administration are insane or completely ignorant regarding Iran and their global radical intentions or deliberately attempting to weaken the ability of the United States to effectively deal with global/trouble spots especially in the Middle East. Iran's citizens were chanting in the streets death to Israel and death to America, WHILE our representative, Secretary of State

John Kerry was signing a nuclear agreement giving Iran the ability to develop nuclear weapons. That's the equivalent of giving a crazy person, who has made it very clear he wants to kill everyone in the neighborhood, a machine gun while his family is chanting death to the neighborhood and taking him at his word that he will not use it.

Either Obama hates Israel and the United States or loves Iran. Either way, he, his advisors and since Congress went along with this should all be institutionalized for the insanity!

Speaking of not being able to negotiate why were the four American prisoners held in Iran not part of the negotiations? Do you think they might have been included and released if their last names were Kerry, Obama, Clinton or families of the Washington elite on either side?

Because of these events my patent is needed now more than ever before in America and throughout the world! Iran cannot be clearer on their global intentions of wiping Israel off the map, weakening the United States and causing worldwide chaos and devastation. There is nothing else that will end the potential for war now that Iran has been given the capability to develop nuclear weapons than my patent and it can be done without firing a shot!

Without my patent the world better get ready!

CHAPTER 6

Immigration

As I indicated in my preface I wrote Political Correctness is BS out of frustration, with far-left activist groups that try to force their double standards on the rest of us. Frustrated with our inept political system and the extremely weak leadership that is misleading our country. Immigration is one of these problems that I consider most frustrating.

The United States has immigration laws regarding entry into our country. These laws require documentation for all non-US residents. If you are a visitor, you are required to have a passport. If you want to gain citizenship, you must apply and register. This is known as legal entry. We are no different from our neighbors to the south, Mexico, and to the north, Canada. In fact it is a universal system and it is fair and logical.

The problem is that we, the United States, have never secured our southern border and our politicians are too weak to address the issue and solve the problem. Illegal immigrants are crossing our borders in great numbers and have been doing so for years. Even in the aftermath of 9/11, our political leaders are unwilling to resolve this problem.

Wow! Our leaders are so inept they are encouraging another 9/11 and are too ignorant to know it. The fact is, whether our borders are secure or not, it is illegal to enter our country, without proper documentation. It is like a stranger entering your unlocked home without permission. It is against the law.

Before we examine this issue any further, I want to discuss the role our weak leadership has played in escalating this problem. In the 1970s Mexico had a population explosion. The Mexican government needed to create three million new jobs per year to handle this rise in population but could not do so. The Mexican economic situation was deteriorating and our government knew it and did not increase border security in response.

President Carter was slow to react to most situations and did nothing. Even President Reagan, whom I greatly admire, did not adequately respond. They both knew firsthand that illegal immigrants were crossing our borders and they did not take action to prevent it. The Mexican workers had to eat and were unable to find work in Mexico so they started to illegally cross our borders. Instead of instituting a documented system to handle the increased number of immigrants, our government never reacted.

A documented system would allow us to keep track of everyone who enters our country. This program would have eliminated our current crisis. None of our presidents from Jimmy Carter to President Obama has addressed this situation and, as a result, we have approximately twelve million undocumented people in our country and growing.

The immigration problem was created by illegal immigrants, but exacerbated by our government's unwillingness to react. Immigration gives both parties an opportunity to point fingers and accuse their rivals, which is very important when shifting blame. Both parties are experts in the game of finger pointing and would rather have someone to blame than to alleviate the problem.

Abortion has also compounded the situation. While Mexico's population was increasing, our population was decreasing. With Roe vs. Wade, the US Supreme Court legalized abortion in 1973. Since 1973, there have been close to 50 million abortions. Since 1986, there have been 32.5 million alone. This number has greatly decreased the birth rate in the United States and therefore decreased our potential workforce. This makes it necessary to import foreign labor. Foreign labor is not the problem—illegal labor is, especially since 9/11.

How many of these undocumented illegal immigrants are Muslim terrorists? Our government has no idea. Undocumented immigrants entering are illegal and in violation of our laws and some may be a threat to our society, yet our politicians still sit and do nothing. Every other immigrant entering our country from Europe, Asia, Africa, and so on has had to abide by our laws. These laws are especially important today to monitor entry and help keep the criminal drug dealers and terrorist element out.

We have no idea how many potential terrorists have entered our country waiting to do us harm, and still our government does nothing. They are too busy doing what they do best--arguing among themselves. They are professional finger-pointers and I can't stress this point enough.

The Mexican government, because of a bad economy, is actually encouraging this illegal activity to exist. They are encouraging their citizens to break our laws while making sure no one enters their country without proper documentation. Instead of working together with our government to find a legal solution, they are undermining us. In fact, they have even threatened to sue us if we build walls and increase security to stop the flow of illegal immigration.

Former President Felipe Calderon of Mexico reprimanded Arizona for taking matters into their own hands by passing a law banning illegal entry into our country. Arizona is in a state of panic because of this illegal intrusion. Violent crime is through the roof and its citizens are living in fear of their lives. So what did many of our fearless leaders in Washington do they side with the Mexican President and give him a standing ovation for his comments.

In fact the Obama Administration sued Arizona for passing the law that protects its citizens. The President of Mexico is way out of line defending illegal entry into our country when those entering are breaking our laws.

I am sure he would view the situation differently if there were 12 million illegal Americans in Mexico draining their economy. The far left loved Calderon and I viewed him as a big bag of wind trying to employ a double standard.

Besides he should have focused all his attention on the crime being committed by the Mexican drug cartels. Murder of police officers in Mexico, continues to be at an all-time high as well as the murder of its citizens in general. Mexico because of the increase in crime is in complete cachous. Strong effective leaders improve their situation before lecturing to others. That's why I called him a blow hard.

The Mexican government continues to undermine us even further by supplying maps indicating the best means of entry into our country. They supply food and water to the illegal immigrants for their journey. The Mexican government also accuses the United States of being racist because we are trying to secure our borders and keep our country safe. What audacity! To accuse America of racism, for trying to secure our borders, yet it is against the law in Mexico to enter that country without proper documentation. Hypocrisy anyone, it's again a case of do as I say, not as I do.

The immigrant leadership in the United States has been conducting huge demonstrations in our country in support of these workers. When you do something illegal, you are a criminal. If you aid a known criminal, that is illegal. Yet the Mexican-American leadership does it every day without ever being prosecuted. I guess for some reason they feel our laws do not apply to them. Organizations like the ACLU defend this nonsense.

Let me give you an example. In Los Angles, the immigrant workers and their supporters staged a huge rally in support of illegal immigrants. The rally got violent and police used force to restore order. As a result, many police officers have been removed for excessive force. The ACLU, of course is supporting the workers. Many in the march threw objects at police and were there to cause trouble. The police, not the criminals, are now under investigation. **In my opinion, the protected ACLU is the greatest ally criminals have ever had.**

It is beyond belief that foreign lawbreakers demonstrate in our streets against our country and it is the police who are considered the problem. Wrong has become right and right has become wrong. Our political leaders should hang their heads in shame. They are being ridiculed and laughed at by criminals, terrorists, and those that support them and say little or nothing in return.

These illegal immigrants are supported by many politicians,

newspaper reporters, and television journalists. Politicians are supposed to be encouraging enforcement of our laws and the media is supposed to be unbiased in their reporting of the news. Instead, it is the opposite.

The television journalist with the most biased view of the immigration situation is Geraldo Rivera of Fox news and I love Fox News. He will defend any Hispanic who crosses our borders. When some commit crimes he is never outraged, no matter how horrific the crime. To achieve his Hispanic agenda he will defend all immigrants in their illegal activities. Fox news is always complaining about network affiliates being biased, and it is Geraldo, one of their own, who is the most biased. Geraldo Rivera is not a journalist he is an activist posing as a journalist regarding this matter.

Not only are his reports slanted in favor of illegal immigration, he is a lawyer and should understand that the solution to the immigration problem will become a precedent. If illegal immigrants from Mexico can cross our borders and receive amnesty, then anyone can enter our country illegally, assuring another 9/11. How can you tell one group of immigrants that they do not need to be documented but every other immigrant from other countries do?

He is allowing his agenda to interfere with logic. Geraldo even wanted the illegal immigrants now in our country to have their families join them in the United States. It is like a double reward, giving amnesty for their illegal entry and then rewarding them by allowing their families to join them. I wonder if Geraldo would defend Americans who crossed illegally into Mexico with as much biased vigor. Hannity, whom I greatly admire and Geraldo are friends so hopefully they will come up with a mutual solution based on logic not emotion!

They are both very smart!

Our political leaders who address this issue and try to uphold the law are often criticized for their efforts. Their political rivals consider them politically incorrect or racist. Because this issue has never been resolved, we have, as I said, approximately twelve million illegal aliens in our country. We have no idea how many are violent criminals or terrorists until they violate our citizens. When they do, rest assure that the ACLU will be there to assist them.

Politicians like Nancy Pelosi and Chuck Schumer are very much in favor illegal entry. If they along with the Democratic Party can help the illegal immigrants gain citizenship it would become a powerful voting block as I stated earlier. They have little to no compassion for the people of Arizona and are only interested in the votes. I previously made a prediction that the Democrats under the Obama administration would try to pass an amnesty bill. I don't know about you but this type of smoke and mirror deception is not the change I was looking for. Isn't it the equivalent of selling your soul for votes?

I have a letter that was sent to President Obama by Arizona Governor Janice K. Brewer dated: June 23, 2010, regarding this matter. It is 4 pages long so I will try to summarize its content.

The Governor starts the letter by thanking the President for meeting with her. She goes onto say that her constituents reported that new signs were posted warning Arizona residents not to access federal lands due to criminal activity associated with the border. These warnings signal to residents that portions of the border have been handed over to illegal immigrants and drug traffickers. She said instead we should be warning international law breakers that they will be detained and prosecuted.

In the next paragraph she discusses the commitment the President made for National Guard troops but she is still waiting on the specific details of deployment. The governor goes on to say, "I strongly urge you to request your staff to provide me with the missing details of your proposal."

The governor has proposed a four point Border Surge strategy.

1. Deploy National Guard Personnel and Aviation which will support federal, state and local law enforcement. They will serve as a blocking force to stop illegal crossing activities. Employ the troops and that will speak loudly to all both north and south of the border that the U.S. is serious about illegal entry.

2. Border fence must be completed reinforced and maintain. This will minimize illegal entry.

3. Enforce Federal Law and Appropriately Fund the Effort. The USA must be prepared to detain, prosecute and then incarcerate convicted violators of United States laws. The governor is still requesting specific details.

4. Reimburse States for the Additional Burden of Illegal Immigration. She needs federal money to cover state prison costs of $150 million along with law enforcement, prosecution and defense costs and health care. Arizona is currently hundreds of millions of dollars short and she says it is unfair for taxpayers to carry these burdens. Especially since the dollars are going to illegal aliens.

In conclusion she says "Finally I want to re-extend the

invitation I made to you to come to Arizona yourself, visit with families living along the southwest border and see the situation firsthand. My prior visit to the border and the air survey of the Cochise County region, have been very important to shaping my perspectives and thinking. Former Governor Richardson joined me for one trip and I believe you will also benefit from such an experience."

"And when you come lunch is on me!"

Signed: Janice K. Brewer Governor

In the letter I could feel her passion. The situation in Arizona is a desperate one and their citizen are in fear. But that means little to nothing to many of our fearless leaders. If President Obama does not go there and try to improve the situation first hand I will be very disappointed. Since he has decided to sue Arizona for doing the federal government's job he and his administration are disgraceful.

This issue on immigration again indicates that our laws pertain to some and not all. Those that are supported by loud and aggressive activist groups strike fear in the hearts and minds of our so called "leaders." If both parties cannot resolve this issue, how do we expect them to ever resolve any issue? If it is the law, enforce it! That's called leadership101!

We have the technology to put an astronaut on the moon yet cannot monitor our borders. We are replacing logic and truth with political correctness. Many of our so-called leaders are afraid to take a stand on anything that is controversial, and this is creating a dangerous situation for all Americans.

Our borders are not secure, and criminals and terrorists know it. If we have another 9/11, and I am afraid that is a real possibility, our politicians will be pointing at each other. When they do we should give them and the ACLU mirrors so the can place the blame where it really belongs.

I want to say that I am not against Mexican workers coming to the United States. I just want them to obey our laws by entering legally. Our country's security depends on it. The vast majority of Mexican workers crossing our borders are hard-working, citizens with strong family ties, and we need their labor. Remember, Mexico would not tolerate illegal entry into their country and neither should we. It is not safe in our post-9/11 world and it's very expensive.

Sometimes groups think if they shout loudly enough and often enough they will accomplish their goals. This is happening because the immigrant leadership is strong and organized and our leadership, if that is what you want to call it, is not. That does not make them right it just makes them successful in distorting the truth. In light of 9/11, we, as Americans, look to our leaders to uphold our Constitution and protect us from foreign invasion. Our borders need to be secured immediately, to ensure our safety.

To fix this problem we should join together, Republican and Democrat (if that is possible), and define a strategy that would close both borders permanently, as Governor Brewer requested. The strategy would coincide with Governor Brewers four point border surge strategy, which includes Air support and mobilizing the National Guard to work together with the border patrol. If our border patrol feels threatened at any time, it must have the ability to defend itself, as it sees fit, without fear of reprisal from far left activist groups and their lawyers.

Since we need their labor, we must find all illegal

immigrants and try to help them become legal documented citizens, which will require them to pay into the system by way of taxes, healthcare etc. As I stated earlier, most Mexican immigrants are terrific workers and we want to encourage them to stay here legally. But they must go to the back of the line and wait a number of years for voting privileges. This will insure that our vote crazy politicians will not immediately benefit. We must never reward those that break our laws.

Any immigrant with a violent criminal record must be located, incarcerated, or deported. We should also include the Mexican government in our discussion and let them see our willingness to resolve this problem fairly, always staying strong in our convictions. We are not wrong when we enforce our laws and protect our citizens.

Immigration is an easy problem to fix with strong, decisive leadership. The immigration problem still being unresolved is an indication of weak leadership. We as Americans have the power to vote the strong and ethical into office just as we have the ability to vote out the weak. Let's use that power to help secure our country. Once again John F. Kennedy said, "Every man-made problem has a man-made solution." We are in need of leaders like JFK and Ronald Reagan. There is a solution to this problem if our leaders come together and have the courage to solve it fairly.

In conclusion common sense dictates: If you want to find a worthwhile career and not be stuck in a menial job speak the language of the country you reside in. If you live in Spain speak Spanish if you live in France learn French and if you are in America and want to reap the benefits of Americas vast opportunities speak English. Anyone who tells you different is not providing you good advice.

Example: "It is my humble opinion that you cannot be a faithful patriotic citizen if you cannot speak the language of the country you live in." Quang Nguyen, Vietnamese refugee now a US citizen. By the way he entered our country legally!

CHAPTER 7

New Religious Alliance

This chapter focuses on Christians and Jews uniting and why I feel it is imperative at this time in history. To do this I must continue to discuss and explore the evils of terrorism. I have stated that many non-Muslims throughout our world seem to be oblivious to the seriousness of this situation. In fact on the contrary I feel that many people worldwide are becoming anti Semitic and it frightens me.

The UN which I consider a joke is always ready to condemn Israel for their behavior when they are simply trying to survive in a hostile region and remain silent regarding the Muslims and the terror they employ. I am very pro-Israel because they are trying to live in peace next door to an enemy that has vowed to annihilate them. We have a former President of the United States, Jimmy Carter supposedly a devout Christian making what I consider anti-Semitic statements.

The Obama administration also seemed to be unaware of the explosive environment around them because they had appointed two devout Muslims to homeland security. They are Arif Alikhan who became assistant secretary for policy development and Kareem Shora who was ADC National Director as a member of the homeland security advisory council. Both are admitted devout Muslims.

To me the difference between good and evil cannot be clearer. In this chapter I will first draw a parallel between Christianity and the Jewish faith while continuing to draw attention on the Muslim situation because the truth must be told.

In Mathew 5:44, God instructs Christians to "love your enemies, and pray for those who persecute you." Christians are commanded to peacefully interact with Christians and non-Christians. It is a testament to our faith. Compare these teachings to those of the Muslim fundamentalists, who feel they are instructed by God to kill all non-Muslims.

I have always judged people by their actions and ideology. For any Muslim to feel justified in the killing of another human being, for simply not being Muslim is very troubling. It is against everything that I consider moral and humane. The world must stand together to destroy those who are brainwashed in this ideology and commit these atrocities. I am convinced that Christians and Jews united are the only ones that are strong enough to lead this effort.

Christian and Jews have had to tolerate each other for 2,000 years. Although they have much in common, they have never had a reason to unite until now. When we examine Christianity, we see that it was originally a Jewish movement. Every writer in the Old and New Testament was Jewish except for Luke who was a Greek doctor. All of Jesus Christ's disciples were Jewish.

St. Paul, who wrote most of the New Testament, was a devout Jew. Christian salvation is guaranteed through the death and resurrection of Jesus Christ, a Jew. **The Christian faith is based on a Jewish messiah.**

Yet down through the centuries there has been a lot of friction between Christians and Jews. The Spanish Inquisition resulted in the deaths of thousands of Jews, simply for not converting to Catholicism. As a result of this and other acts of discrimination, many Jews have felt an alliance only toward other Jews.

Before 9/11, I felt that Israel was responsible for most of the strife in the Middle East. I had compassion for the Palestinian situation and felt that Israel was the unprovoked aggressor. The land that Israel took from Palestine after the Six Day' War should be returned, or so I thought. This was my position prior to 9/11.

The events that occurred on 9/11 and after have convinced me that I was wrong. Israel is dealing with a fanatical religious fundamentalist group that is dedicated to Israel's destruction. In fact, as I stated earlier this fanatical group is dedicated to the annihilation of everyone who is not Muslim. When I see these fanatics justify the bombing of innocent men, women, and children in the name of Allah, it gives me a completely different perspective of the situation. Especially, when they tie explosives to their own children and use them as human sacrifices.

I have never heard of any Christian or Jewish group that would sacrifice their children in the name of God. Moral and ethical people could never condone such suicidal behavior. The Islamic fundamentalists are at war with all non-Muslims. They are prepared to commit the most horrific acts to achieve world dominance. They hate Christians and Jews and are dedicated in establishing a new world order with Muslims in charge. Their form of morality is convoluted and against everything our Judeo-Christian culture believes.

In London there was a demonstration by the so called moderate Muslims, confirming this fanaticism. It was ironically enough called, "the religion of peace demonstration." The following signs were carried by these self-proclaimed, "peaceful" demonstrators. This supposedly peaceful Islamic religious gathering will give you some idea of the lunatics we are dealing with. Judge for yourself whether you think anyone could interpret these signs as messages of peace.

- MASSACRE THOSE WHO INSULT ISLAM
- BEHEAD THOSE WHO INSULT ISLAM
- EUROPE IS A CANCER ISLAM IS THE ANSWER
- EXTERMINATE THOSE WHO SLANDER ISLAM
- ISLAM WILL DOMINATE THE WORLD
- FREEDOM GO TO HELL
- EUROPE, TAKE SOME LESSONS FROM 9/11
- EUROPE, YOU WILL PAY—YOUR 9/11 IS ON IT'S WAY
- SLAY THOSE WHO INSULT ISLAM
- BE PREPARED FOR THE REAL HOLOCAUST

I know that in previous chapters I have empathically discussed the Muslim situation but I do so because I think this self proclaimed "religion of peace" is waging war on the free world. I feel they are an enemy that we will have to deal with in the future and many Americans, I believe, are unaware of the threat they pose, including former President Obama.

As the demonstrator's signs indicate England as well as America better be prepared because they have vowed that England will be the first country they take over. The British government better be ready to fight fire with fire or face some terrible consequences.

Why weren't these hateful demonstrations shown on network television or in our major newspapers? Could it be that the mainstream media is becoming so far left that they would risk another disaster rather than confirm that there is a real war on terror? Remember Mark Twain said "When you don't read the newspaper your uninformed, if you do read the newspaper you're misinformed." Many in the media today are far left and want to slant the news rather than report the news.

It is because of Islam that Christians and Jews must unite to defeat this common and deadly enemy. This alliance is necessary for both religions, as well as all non-Muslims, to survive.

For many years, the evangelical Christians have shown great support for Israel. Former Prime Minister Menachem Begin used to visit Reverend Jerry Falwell on his trips to the United States. They would discuss how the Bible and the Christian and Jewish faiths were so closely intertwined in the future of the Middle East. The following is a Publishers Weekly review of Zev Chafets's book that supports the need for this alliance.

A Match Made in Heaven: American Jews, Christian Zionists, and One Man's Exploration of the Weird and Wonderful Judeo-Evangelical Alliance.

"In this provocative study, Chafets, a journalist and former Menachem Begin press secretary, explores American evangelical support for Israel. Chafets interweaves reflections on the history of American Christians' embrace of Israel with contemporary reporting, visiting places like Jerry Falwell's Liberty University and tagging along on an evangelical tour of the Holy Land. Perhaps his most important point is that, despite American reporters' claims that only Israeli fanatics have accepted evangelical support, in fact "mainstream Israel" has welcomed the alliance. Chafets argues that especially in a time of war, American Jews need to realize that it is "Muslim fascists," not evangelical Christians, who are Israel's enemy. He acknowledges that much Christian Zionism includes belief in an end-times scenario in which Jews do not fare well, but asks why Jews should care so much about their place in Christian eschatology, since Jews reject Christian accounts of the end times tout court. Altogether, Chafets's portrait suggests a great gulf between American Jewry and Israelis, and also points to great diversity of views among American Christians: liberal Protestants tend to be more equivocal in their support of Israel. This intensely readable book, which ends with a warning that evangelical enthusiasm for Israel ought not to be taken for granted and is sure to spark heated debate."

We must now form this religious alliance because it seems that most of the world has turned against Israel and the United States. Even many of our colleges in our own country are anti Jewish and Christian. Many seem to be very sympathetic to the Islamic fundamentalist cause. These far-left groups are against the traditional values that most of us hold dear. Such as: The far left ACLU that defends suspected terrorist even when they know their clients maybe a great danger to our country. I consider them anti-American when they fight for the release of suspected terrorists that are being held in Guantanamo Bay even when our national security is at risk.

Far left entertainers who compare Christian fundamentalist

with Muslim fundamentalists have a misguided value system that most Americans oppose. Every country that has turned away from Israel is also becoming anti United States and many in our own country are doing the same. These misguided individuals see us as the aggressor, not the Islamic fundamentalists. This is astonishing to me.

Many in our society do not feel threatened by the Islamic fundamentalists because they feel they are only responding to our occupation of Iraq. They think that when we leave Iraq and Afghanistan the terrorist situation will go away. I know they were greatly mistaken. It is a religious issue, as I have said repeatedly, with these Islamic terrorists, not a land issue. To emphasize this point I addressed specific Muslim acts of world terrorism prior to 9/11 in the terrorist chapter of this book.

These fanatics hate everyone who is not Muslim. They do not care who these non-Muslims are or what good they have done for humanity. They especially hate Christians and Jews for simply being non-Muslim. They are indiscriminate in their terrorist targets. They will kill men, women, and children in the name of Allah. They are a threat to our entire civilization, as we know it. If the United States is going to survive, we must come together as a nation and realize the dangerous situation we face.

Instead, our political parties do not help because they hate each other with such passion and are always trying to undermine each other in every situation. Our political parties are such rivals I think that they would rather have our enemies win than show a united front. I have always said that I am not as concerned about the party in power, Republican or Democrat, as I am with the party seeking power. Politicians will use every devious trick necessary to gain power. They will deny their illegal activities while always accusing their rivals when they engage in similar activities. For this reason, coming together as a united America may be a lot harder than it seems. In fact, in our present situation it may be impossible.

This holy war is forcing Christians and Jews to form a religious alliance. To be effective this alliance must have a strategic plan. As a Christian and an American,

I have a great interest in seeing this alliance succeed. The preservation of our Judeo-Christian culture depends on it. To ensure this success I recommend we do the following:*

- We must recognize the Islamic fundamentalist threat. As I said, I feel the majority of nonMuslims around the world do not take this threat seriously. History should have taught us a lesson with Nazi Germany. If the world had confronted the Germans before they became a world power, World War II could have possibly been avoided. This situation with the Muslims can only get worse if not confronted.

- Immediately stop all Muslim immigration into the United States. We have no idea if the Muslims seeking entry into our country are Islamic fanatics. We cannot afford to take a chance with the lives of our loved ones.

- Find and deport any Muslims suspected of subversive activities. These are dangerous times and we should error on the side of caution.

- We should suspend all civil rights for suspected Muslims terrorists. Our flawed judicial system is being used against us. We must level the playing field and not let our freedoms defeat us. Extreme times call for extreme measures, strength and courage.

- Unity is the key. We cannot be defeated by anyone but ourselves. Democrats and Republican must unite and focus on the real threat to world peace. We must be committed to a strategy that will successfully protect our country and Israel. Our Islamic enemy should see a united uncompromising front. United with Israel we stand, divided we fall.

- The United States and Israel must create a united world force with Europe, China and Russia focused specifically on the terrorist issue. Our Islamic enemy should understand the consequences of their actions if this madness continues. Islam hates everyone who is not Muslim. All non-Muslims should unite and demonstrate a willingness to confront and defeat this religious tyranny.

- We must stay strong with our traditional values and never compromise them. Our Constitution states that we are all created equal. In spite of all our problems, we are still the greatest country in the world. We have a lot to protect and should not be intimidated by anyone.

The new religious alliance is necessary for the preservation of our two religions as well as all of humanity. We must recognize that this is a religious war over religious ideology not territory. We must continue to stress to the non-Muslim world that the terrorist ideology eliminates everyone who is not an Islamic Muslim fundamentalist.

I believe that Christians and Jews must unite now more than ever. Our very survival depends on each other. I pray this alliance will last forever; we have a lot in common. Our values and our view of the world are similar, especially when it comes to human rights and the preservation of life. Our Judeo-Christian values have made our world a better place.

Let us be diligent and protect them.

    *Most important employ my pork weapon strategy, as presented at the end of the terrorism chapter, for the safety and well being of humanity!

CHAPTER 8

Hatred Damages the Soul

Just as I prefaced my preface I want to reiterate that I love diversity and people of all colors and ethnicity and want us all to live together in harmony. In my book I chose to discuss controversial subjects that most in our society are afraid to discuss. These subjects can arouse great emotion and passion. I chose to challenge many on the far left because they are trying to force an ideology that the majority in our country, rejects.

Because I am very passionate defending free speech I may be coming across as very aggressive with my analogies. I can assure you that I have many friends that are on the left as well as center and right. What we all have in common is we respect each others opinions enough to listen. I do not hate anyone but I have real concerns that we as Americans are giving up our ability to think for ourselves because of far left activist intimidation and it concerns me.

Many on the far left preach hatred with those that do not agree with them. The way they ridiculed Sarah Palin and her family to include her mentally challenged son is disgraceful. Hatred is a very strong and damaging emotion. It is so strong that it can paralyze your thought process. It prevents those who hate from being able to effectively communicate and think logically. People that hate attract people who hate—it is a vicious cycle.

In politics, we witness daily how our two-party system

promotes and encourages hatred. The parties are so obsessed with winning they cannot conduct meaningful campaigns based on their accomplishments. Instead, they have to engage in vicious character assassinations designed to destroy their rivals not just defeat them. Their lust for power and money force them to jeopardize their very souls. Each party accuses the other of cheating and lying while each overlooks its own party's criminal behavior. Our two political parties have divided our country more than our enemies could ever do. In fact, they exhibit such hatred toward each other it makes me wonder if they want America to win or America's enemies to win. Many in both parties are hypocrites disguising themselves as patriots.

The problem is compounded because politics attracts young gullible volunteers who are negatively influenced by this behavior. They enter politics as well intended idealists who believe in the strong principles and character of their desired candidate. They listen to and believe their every word. Being young, they are influenced easily by the rhetoric and blinded by their loyalty. This has caused many of them to become obsessed with the destruction of the opposition party.

This is not healthy and creates hateful political paranoia. It also helps to create far-left radicals, whose ideology is distorted. This is having a very negative impact on the future of our country. The far-left ideology is flawed, because it is biased and based on half-truths. This results in a distorted view of right and wrong. When they focus their hatred on their political rivals as their enemy, they will become obsessed with their destruction. Destroying one party in favor of another will lead to our eventual demise.

There is an old saying, "When the elephants fight the ants

take a hell of a beating." When our two parties are fighting, we all suffer. We as citizens are the ants and the growing division between our two parties is beating the hell out of us. Hatred takes precedence over common sense and decency.

I thought there had never been more evidence of this than the hatred displayed by the far left for former President George W. Bush and then President Trump came along. I have never seen this type of hatred not only by the far left but also by their supporters in the main stream media! It's disgraceful! Not agreeing with a president's policy is one thing, and I often have not agreed, but hating him or any of our Presidents with this type of passion is not healthy in a democracy. Our democracy does not benefit when our nation is hopelessly divided. I believe, unfortunately, the media is the primary cause of this hatred!

Disagreeing with a president on the other hand is healthy and is a testament to our democracy; hating them by always trying to undermine them is not. Our flawed Iraq policy was one of the biggest reasons so many disliked our former president. America's decision to invade Iraq was, at best questionable; our occupation of Iraq was a miscalculated disaster. It gave those who love to hate a great excuse to vilify the former president.

Regarding former President Bush I believe another reason so many in our country consider former President Bush to be such a villain, is that he was elected in 2000 without a majority of the popular vote. He did not have the support of the majority of Americans, and his decision to invade Iraq escalated the situation. Whatever the reason, this hatred for him damaged our country by emboldening our enemy. Now it's happening again with President Trump.

Hatred is a damaging emotion that affects your soul. When it becomes out of control, it can negatively affect an entire nation. The division of our two parties has left America very weak and vulnerable. We focus our efforts on the negative instead of working together to the benefit of our citizens.

Hatred is universal in its scope and is certainly not confined to the United States. In fact, Islam is the world's greatest example of how hatred damages the soul. As we have discussed many times already Islam's hatred is, unfortunately, based on religion and it is very confusing. On the one hand, they preach the power and goodness of Allah while they commit deadly acts of terrorism in his name. They kill innocent men, women, and children whose only crime is that they are not Muslim. This type of hatred is impossible for normal people to comprehend. It takes hatred to its lowest level.

In England and Scotland we witnessed how hateful and evil these terrorists can be. In both countries, there were unsuccessful terrorist attempts within hours of each other. They targeted a busy entertainment district in London and the Glasgow airport in Scotland. They chose two places where thousands of people gather. If successful, the terrorists would have killed and injured large groups of innocent people, which was their diabolical plan. The captured terrorists included six Muslim doctors. Doctors who take the Hippocratic Oath to save lives were there to destroy lives. Their insanity allows them to commit these horrendous atrocities in the name of God. Their God is certainly not the God I pray to.

After the failed terrorist attempt, Swedish terrorist expert Magnus Ranstrop was quoted as saying, "There is nothing about being a doctor or highly educated that is inconsistent with being an extremist." If this is true, the United Kingdom has a huge problem and here is why. The United Kingdom's National Health Service employs almost 90,000, doctors who received their medical degrees from foreign countries. Almost 14,000 of these doctors are Muslim.

The question British officials have got to be asking themselves is, "Were these doctors who participated in the recently failed terrorist attacks, already committed Islamic terrorists before arriving in England, or did they receive their indoctrination in local mosques once they arrived?" I would venture a guess that it was probably a little of both. If they were not terrorists when they arrived, they were certainly prime candidates to be further brainwashed and recruited. If this is true, England not only has an immigration problem they also have a homegrown terrorist problem.

The United States has a similar problem regarding foreign doctors. One out of every four doctors practicing in the United States is a graduate from a foreign medical school. More than ten thousand foreign-educated medical students applied for a residency program in the United States. Thirty percent of those who applied are from India and Pakistan. Both countries have huge Muslim populations.

The protected idealists in England and in the United States better understand the seriousness of this Muslim situation before it is too late. Worrying about their civil rights is the last thing we should be concerned with because if we are unable to trust Muslim doctors, what Muslims can be trusted?

If we cannot determine the loyalty of the Muslims who reside in the United States, we should seriously consider deporting all Muslims, unless they are willing to pledge allegiance to our country. The problem in England as well as in the United States is the so-called moderate Muslims remain silent and rarely condemn terrorist violence. Their silence speaks volumes. Do they share the same hatred for both of our countries as the committed terrorists do?

In both of our countries, I would institute a love us or leave us campaign. Especially in light of the recent attacks in England. Can you imagine any other culture or religion where medical doctors would try to kill innocent people in the name of their religion?

That type of hatred is impossible for moral people to comprehend. Yet, it is glorified in the Islamic fundamentalist culture. Those who participate in this treachery have crossed over to the dark side and have no souls. They have no place in a civilized society.

I feel there are three reasons why most people hate.

They are ignorance, fanaticism and frustration. Those who hate out of ignorance are dangerous because they are so difficult to reason with. Many in the Islamic faith are very uneducated and have been indoctrinated (brainwashed), into their beliefs, by manipulative, preacher-like con artists who seek loyal demonic followers. Mindless robots, is a more accurate term for it. These preachers preach hate and violence as a means to an end. They promise their followers virgins in heaven for their evil deeds. No acts of violence are beyond the realm of possibility and those who follow these dictates are mindless criminals.

Fanaticism is also a key element of the Islamic fundamentalist culture. These demons can even brainwash educated professionals, such as doctors, and enslave their minds. These fanatics become so deranged they cannot determine right from wrong. They become mindless suicide killers destroying everyone they meet. Their evil purpose is to rid the world of all non-Muslims. These fanatics are impossible to negotiate with because they are devoid of logic and common sense. Do you think there seems to be a pattern developing between those that hate and Muslim fundamentalists?

The frustrated can also hate because they did not accomplish their desired agenda. I see this with the political far left in our own country. Many have a socialistic agenda that causes them frustration when they fail to obtain it. Their frustration increases when their hated rivals continue to gain more power. The 2004 presidential re-election of George W. Bush is an example of how this frustration can turn to hatred. When this happens their paranoia increases daily.

To give you an example of how emotional people can get regarding this issue, I was at a pizza party with friends some years ago and we started to discuss politics. I know that is always a bad thing to do but we did it. I think I started the discussion by saying that, in my opinion former President Jimmy Carter was the least effective president in the last hundred years. My neighbor snapped back that he hated George W. Bush and he was the worst president ever. I did not even intend to mention then President Bush in our conversation. I was trying to give an example of government ineptness. My neighbor's hatred for former President Bush made it impossible for him not to include him in a negative political discussion. The discussion ended abruptly. My neighbor is a great person and I really like him but he is so emotionally anti-Bush, that it made the discussion uncomfortable. This type of hatred is prevalent throughout the country and prevents meaningful dialog, which in turn will escalate the problem by discouraging diversity of thought.

The best remedy for overcoming hatred is interactive communication with a goal of tolerance and resolution, always encouraging different opinions. When two groups sit down and calmly discuss a subject it helps them better understand the opposition's points of view. When subjects are framed and discussed, they are less intimidating. When both groups have a better understanding of the opponent's thought process, what and why they believe what they do, they can calmly discuss it. This will bring a human element into the conversation, which should relieve some of the animosity.

Do not try to carry on a logical discussion when someone has an extreme hatred for something or someone. The discussion will frustrate you and irritate them. Hate can eliminate meaningful communication. Just look at the Islamic fundamentalist culture, as an example. Islamic fundamentalism is based on hatred. Trying to negotiate with this type of mentality is impossible. If there was ever a culture that proves how destructive it is to hate, it is the Islamic culture.

To support this fanaticism at any level is to support murder and murders. Islamists may not realize how hate damages their message and their credibility. Prolonged hatred will damage your soul; logic and love will restore it.

CHAPTER 9

Racism Today:
Is it profitable?

I want to emphasize that slavery in America followed by years of racism were unjustifiable and cannot be defended. Slaves started migrating to America in the 1500's long before we gained our independence from England and slavery continued until 1865. The Civil War ended slavery but did not end black oppression.

Africans who were sold into slavery by other Africans endured hardship that most of us cannot imagine. Their families were separated and they were required to work long hours under the most unbelievable conditions known to man.

Even after slavery ended in 1865 black Americans were subjected to unequal treatment and denied the most basic rights that most Americans took for granted. The Civil Rights movement in the 1950"s and 60's were justified and necessary to rectify this unfortunate situation.

Dr. Martin Luther King led the civil rights movement and was an effective black leader. His focus was to aid all those that were oppressed and help them gain their rights as citizens of the United States of America. Dr. King's leadership was noble and righteous. He was a leader that all America could be proud of. He tried and was successful at leveling the playing field.

Dr. King never tried to benefit from racism by trying to

manufacture its existence if it did not exist. In other words he tried to eradicate racism not profit from it. He was an effective leader because he improved the lives and behavior of those he lead. I appreciate Dr. King now more than ever especially when I compare him to today's most notable black "leaders."

Many of today's black leaders are different because they discovered that America is so sensitive to its racist past they can benefit from their guilt and many of them have profited greatly. They try to inject racism even when it does not exist. In this chapter we will explore their methods and determine if they are noble or self serving.

Racism occurs when you discriminate against someone based on the color of his or her skin. Some of today's black leaders have tried to change the meaning of racism to serve their purposes. Their definition is that only those in power can be racists. This allows them to engage in racist activities while absolving themselves of responsibility. These manipulators practice racism while always pointing the finger at others.

Today's Black leaders should stop playing the race card and start playing the responsibility card. Many in our society blame racism for their failures and are encouraged to do so. We hear community leaders, athletes, and politicians claiming racism whenever it is convenient for them to further their agenda. I am convinced that most intelligent, logical people in our society today are not racists.

Some years ago when Joe Torre was manager of the New York Yankees he was accused of racism by then Yankee player Gary Sheffield. Sheffield made disparaging remarks about Torre's treatment of black players. The thing that bothered me most about his comments was that he did not have to prove his allegations. Sheffield made millions of dollars per year and he had the audacity to claim discrimination against the Yankees and their management. Gary Sheffield should get a real job and find out how the rest of us live. It may bring him back to reality.

I am certain of one thing. Many of today's inner city leaders try to accuse others outside their communities of racism. It helps divert attention away from them and their lack of accomplishments and it gives them a great opportunity to point the finger and meet their racist agenda. I wonder if Sheffield has ever thought about giving credit to the white baseball establishment, including his agent, for his great wealth for playing a game.

Many of today's black leaders will come to Sheffield's defense because that is what they do. In fact, they encourage racist accusations. Defending these charges provides them a great living. I am confident that most of these charges are complete B.S. As I will state in the bad behavior section of this book, I feel most people today discriminate against behavior not race. People who demonstrate character and integrity are accepted by the masses.

For many years, I belonged to the SYAC at the Syracuse YMCA. SYAC is a private men's club within the YMCA and has many special features such as pool tables, Jacuzzi, TV room, etc. It costs extra to join and it is well worth it. Many of us who are members of SYAC have formed a special bond with each other.

Some years ago, we had a large influx of black Americans who joined our club. They were a great addition. Men like Will Morgan, Nelson Sayles, Glen and Mike Chandler, and others are great people who help make the SYAC a great place to go. The black and white diversity of the club has been a wonderful experience and has made the SYAC a much better place. I call these guys true friends and I am proud to be associated with them. They have character, integrity, and strong moral values. Men like this would be a great addition to any organization in the country. When we interact with each other, we never look at race—only at the way we treat each other.

I remember when Don Imus, a New York radio talk personality, made some disparaging remarks regarding race and the Rutgers women's basketball team. To paraphrase, he said they looked like whores. His statement caused a tremendous outrage among the entire country—especially the black community. Imus was fired for his remarks and he should have been. In fact, I thought Don Imus should have been fired years ago for his verbal attacks on so many people. People who were unable to defend themselves, because they did not belong to an activist group or an organization that would help them do so.

I was not in any way against his firing, but I find it incredible how upset many of the black leaders were for his remarks. They called him a racist and took this opportunity to say how racist the entire country is. It is astonishing to me that they can become so outraged with Imus for calling black female basketball players whores and say nothing about rap music. The rappers' lyrics are so degrading to black women and continue to get worse. The rappers glorify rape; use the N word continually and most of these so-called leaders remain silent. Rap music glorifies prison, killing of police officers and enslavement of women, yet these leaders remain silent.

Here is a great article by Jason Whitlock that appeared in the *Kansas City Star* April 11, 2007, regarding this Imus issue:

"Imus isn't the real bad guy. Instead of wasting time on an irrelevant shock jock, black leaders need to be fighting a growing gangster culture. Thank you, Don Imus. You've given us (black people) an excuse to avoid our real problem. You've given Al Sharpton and Jesse Jackson another opportunity to pretend that the old fight, which is now the safe and lucrative fight, is still the most important fight in our push for true economic and social equality.

You've given Vivian Stringer and Rutgers the chance to hold a nationally televised recruiting celebration expertly disguised as a news conference to respond to your poor attempt at humor. Thank you, Don Imus. You extended Black History Month to April, and we can once again wallow in victim hood, protest like its 1965, and delude ourselves into believing that fixing your hatred is more necessary than eradicating our self-hatred.

The bigots win again. While we're fixated on a bad joke cracked by an irrelevant, bad shock jock, I'm sure at least one of the marvelous young women on the Rutgers basketball team is somewhere snapping her fingers to the beat of 50 Cent's or Snoop Dogg's or Young Jeezy's latest ode glorifying nappy-headed pimps and hos.

I ain't saying Jesse, Al, and Vivian are gold-diggas, but they don't have the heart to mount a legitimate campaign against the real black-folk killas. It is us. At this time, we are our own worst enemies. We have allowed our youths to buy into a culture (hip hop) that has been perverted, corrupted and overtaken by prison culture. The music, attitude and behavior expressed in this culture is anti-black, anti-education, demeaning, self destructive, pro-drug dealing and violent.

Rather than confront this heinous enemy from within, we sit back and wait for someone like Imus to have a slip of the tongue and make the mistake of repeating the things we say about ourselves.

It's embarrassing. Dave Chappelle was offered $50 million to make racially insensitive jokes about black and white people on TV. He was hailed as a genius.

Black comedians routinely crack jokes about white and black people, and we all laugh out loud. I'm no Don Imus apologist. He and his tiny companion Mike Lupica blasted me after I fell out with ESPN. Imus is a hack.

But, in my view, he didn't do anything outside the norm for shock jocks and comedians. He also offered an apology. That should have been the end of this whole affair. Instead, it's only the beginning. It's an opportunity for Stringer, Jackson, and Sharpton to step on victim platforms and elevate themselves and their agenda$.

I watched the Rutgers news conference and was ashamed. Martin Luther King Jr. spoke for eight minutes in 1963 at the March on Washington. At the time, black people could be lynched and denied fundamental rights with little thought. With the comments of a talk show host most of her players had never heard of before last week serving as her excuse, Vivian Stringer rambled on for 30 minutes about the amazing season her team had.

Somehow, we're supposed to believe that the comments of a man with virtually no connection to the sports world ruined Rutgers' wonderful season. Had a broadcaster with credibility and a platform in the sports world uttered the words Imus did, I could understand a level of outrage.

But an hour-long press conference over a man who has already apologized, already been suspended and is already insignificant is just plain intellectually dishonest. This is opportunism. This is a distraction.

In the grand scheme, Don Imus is no threat to us in general and no threat to black women in particular. If his words are so powerful and so destructive and must be rebuked so forcefully, then what should we do about the idiot rappers on BET, MTV and every black owned radio station in the country who use words much more powerful and much more destructive?

I don't listen or watch Imus' show regularly. Has he at any point glorified selling crack cocaine to black women? Has he celebrated black men shooting each other randomly? Has he suggested in any way that it's cool to be a baby-daddy rather than a husband and a parent? Does he tell his listeners that they're suckers for pursuing education and that they're selling out their race if they do?

When Imus does any of that, call me and I'll get upset. Until then, he is what he is—a washed-up shock jock who is very easy to ignore when you're not looking to be made a victim.

No. We all know where the real battleground is. We know that the gangsta rappers and their followers in the athletic world have far bigger platforms to negatively define us than some old white man with a bad radio show. There's no money and lots of danger in that battle, so Jesse and Al are going to sit it out."

This is a great article for two reasons. It is politically

incorrect and therefore truthful. One usually follows the other. Thank you, Jason Whitlock, for not being afraid to identify the real problem.

When Jason Whitlock said that "the old fight has now become the safe and lucrative fight" that is a very important statement to remember. While Jesse Jackson's net worth has greatly improved those in his community are still struggling. Do you really think he wants to end the perception of racism? He might have to get a real job if he cannot continually prove and benefit from perceived racism in America.

To today's black leaders what is said is not as important as who said it. Most black leaders are interested in only the negative comments of those who are not black. That is what makes them phony leaders. I am not defending Imus; I am saying that many leaders in the black community have no credibility. They look into a magnifying glass at those outside their community who make disparaging remarks and never take issue with those in their community. A community is no different from a corporation or a family: it rots from the inside out.

The ghetto culture is a subculture and instead of helping those in the culture evolve out of it, many leaders within their communities defend the culture verbally or through their silence. When you defend or excuse bad behavior, you are encouraging bad behavior.

In his book Black Rednecks and White Liberals, that I referred to previously, Thomas Sowell, a black American, claims that the black ghetto culture is actually a white cracker culture. The African slaves who settled in the South assimilated into the white cracker culture and adopted it. Sowell says that it was actually a white subculture brought over from northern England. Adopting this cracker culture prevented the southern blacks from growing into a more sophisticated society. He concluded that defending this culture, amounts to endorsing and approving destructive behavior.

There are still many whites who live in this cracker culture. The difference is you do not hear white leaders with an ounce of credibility defending or encouraging this behavior unless, as I said, they are just bad leaders.

Most societies evolve and become more sophisticated as time goes on. Helping those around you to be the best they can be, and going to the next level is positive leadership. Looking at your community first for improvement before condemning everyone else outside your community is strong, constructive leadership. Leadership starts in the home. When there is strong leadership in the home, children and communities benefit.

I have a real good black friend who is a good example of this. Ronald "Otis" Jennings was brought up in the Bronx in New York City. Otis told me that when he was growing up in the Bronx many black leaders blamed white America for everything that went wrong in their lives. It was negatively affecting his view of white people until his mother gave him some great wisdom that changed his perception. Mrs. Jennings, told Otis, "Do not be fooled—the devil comes in all colors." In other words, there are good and bad people in all races.

Leaders improve the lives of those they lead; they do not blame everyone outside their family or community for the problems in their community. Otis has become a very kind and sophisticated adult with great values and perceptions. He is a great father, husband, friend, and a productive member of society.

Many black leaders look to their community's lack of accomplishments and blame racism. They never blame themselves or their communities. It is politically correct to blame the white establishment for all their failures. That is bad leadership and it is very destructive to those they lead. Community leaders must take some responsibility for their communities' lack of success. If not, their communities will never improve.

There are other black leaders emerging who stress personal responsibility. People like Thomas Sowell, Star Parker and more that focus on what black Americans need to do to help themselves. If the majority of the black leadership adopted Thomas Sowell's, a former liberals philosophies, the black community would improve. I believe there is tremendous talent waiting to flourish in these communities. Under new leadership, the economic gap between black and white would narrow substantially.

If someone has been a recognized leader for twenty plus years in any business or community with very little to show in social or economic improvement—he or she should be replaced. If racism and poverty are still flourishing in these communities then maybe they have the wrong leaders in charge. How long do they get to fail? Bad leaders accomplish little and blame everyone else for their failure.

Racism is as much about economics as it is about color. Great leaders help improve the economic situation of those they lead. That is what makes them great leaders. Their philosophies and actions stress personal responsibility. They condemn those in their community who are destructive whether it is in their music or their behavior. Crime in their community will gradually go down. They will stress education and strong work ethics. They will help create an environment where great effort in work or school is encouraged.

As I stated earlier leaders should be judge on one primary criterion those under their leadership have improved their skills and behavior. Everything else is secondary. Strong positive leadership will help transform the black community from victims to achievers by adopting an "if it is to be it is up to me" attitude among each member of the community.

An amazing individual with that "if it is to be it is up to me" attitude is Star Parker. Her personal transformation from the Los Angles welfare roles to conservative crusader has been chronicled by ABC's 20/20 as well as other news sources and is very inspiring.

She went from welfare to accepting Christianity to receiving a BS degree in marketing to launching an urban Christian magazine. Ms. Parker is the founder and president of CURE, the Center for Urban Renewal and Education. Her focus is on faith and marketing based alternatives to empower the lives of the poor. She is a great success and true leader.

An old African proverb states, "It takes an entire village to raise a child." That is great wisdom, as long as the community or village is a place where a child can grow and flourish. The leaders in these communities should be beyond reproach, always trying to set a good example. They should encourage good performance and discipline bad behavior.

All leaders who have been in power for many years should be judged on this criterion. Most credible leaders are elected by their districts, not self-appointed. Unfortunately, many leaders of the black community are self-proclaimed leaders and continue to gain prominence and increase their net worth because of their ability to blame others for their communities' lack of growth.

Has Jesse Jackson or Al Sharpton, ever been elected to their positions as America's black voice? If they have they better hope they can continue to blame racism on everything that goes wrong for black people in our country. If not, they should have to explain their role and the lack of leadership they have provided for so many years. What responsibility does black leadership take in their communities' lack of growth? It cannot always be someone else's fault.

I have created a list on how to identify racism. My racist meter will show you how to identify a racist community leader, organization or individual. Racists will:

• Deny employment on the sole basis of race always generalize when making racist accusations

• Physically violate those entering their neighborhoods on basis of skin color

• Change their criteria when they or their community is accused of racism

• Always accuse others of racism when caught in a compromising position

• Always defend their race regardless of the situation and position themselves as victims

- Never give credit for the good provided them, they feel entitled

- Never take responsibility for their communities' high crime rates

- Blame all their communities failures on racism, never taking responsibility

I have always said that the best way to identify a racist is when you hear someone always accusing everyone else of racism. As I previously said, some black leaders have gone so far as to say that black people cannot be racist because only those in power have the ability to discriminate. What a bunch of BS. You are a racist if you discriminate based on color period. And you are a con artist to imply anything else.

When people are physically assaulted, resulting in injury or death based solely on skin color, they have no power. They were violated by racists and those who try to justify these actions by reversing their standards are themselves racists, hypocrites. Those who practice this con game make a living on distorting the truth. Many on the far left encourage the distortion and that makes it even more pathetic. One group lies and the other group swears to it.

Racism is a great excuse for failed leadership.

CHAPTER 10

Real Leadership Eliminates Bad Behavior

As we discussed in the previous chapter real leaders improve the skills and behavior of those they lead. They will discipline nonperformance while celebrating and encouraging outstanding achievement. They never lower their standards regarding performance or make excuses to accommodate those not performing. Bad behavior is never justified or defended. When bad behavior is defended, bad behavior is encouraged.

Unfortunately we witnessed first hand how excusing bad behavior only encourages additional bad behavior. In this example the bad behavior I am referring to is the murderous behavior by Joran Vander Sloot of Aruba. With the help of his now deceased father and his defense attorney he was allowed to make a further mockery of the already flawed judicial system.

Joran was a prime suspect in the disappearance and assumed death of Natalee Holoway and was never brought to trial because of the loop holes in what I refer to as the "injustice system." His father and his attorney did everything they could to manipulate the system so he could avoid prosecution. Joran was released and as a result 5 years later a 21 year old Peruvian woman was murdered. Joran has confessed to her murder.

It's a clear example of when bad /murderous behavior is defended it is encouraged. I blamed his farther as much as I do him. They are both despicable.

I have long thought that most clear-thinking and logical people are not prejudiced against race. They become prejudiced against bad behavior especially when that behavior, no matter how bizarre, is defended.

The biggest problem in overcoming racial stereotyping is compounded with bad leadership. When those in leadership roles defend the bad behavior of those they lead, they are sending a message that they and their communities look beyond their own actions and focus on the reactions of people outside their communities. This creates a hostile environment when an individual's behavior is justified in spite of the seriousness of the offense.

We witness some professional inner-city athletes who act like thugs. These high-priced professional athletes will give their gang signs on national television for all their loyal impressionable fans to see. Many of them come from an undisciplined subculture that promotes and encourages bad behavior that goes unchallenged by their parent, parents, or community leaders. Defending and justifying this culture has had a very negative effect on our youth.

These are the same athletes and leaders who are always accusing everyone else of racism when their behavior is challenged. Responsible people in our society should always discriminate against bad behavior. It is the responsible thing to do. The problem is that most community leaders change their standards regarding behavior when it affects them or their communities. They always have good excuses when their communities are involved in negative situations.

Let me give you an example how some of these phony leaders change their standards. Remember when Michael Vick, the former Atlanta Falcons quarterback, was accused of animal cruelty. It was alleged then confirmed that he and some of his friends had a dog-fighting ring on Michael Vick's property. The allegations went on to say the brutality did not stop there. They destroyed some of the losing dogs by drowning or slamming them to the ground until they died. The evidence was overwhelming, pointing to Vick and his associates. This is brutal behavior at the subhuman level.

I wanted to see how many of those black leaders who accused the Duke Lacrosse players of rape without one shred of evidence would react to the Michael Vick situation. I predicted that they would either come to Vick's defense and accuse the prosecutor of racism or remain silent. Those who remained silent did so because they said Vick is innocent until proven guilty. This is the opposite of what they said in the Duke Lacrosse case.

It just proves that these phony leaders are more interested in who committed the crime rather than the crime committed. That is why I say bad leadership causes discrimination and racial strife, because they are biased when judging bad behavior in their communities.

I first witnessed this many years ago during the Watts riots, many black leaders, blamed everyone but the rioters. When rioters were caught shooting at police and burning down stores, many community leaders focused on the forceful reaction of police. Many blamed the police more than the rioters. These are the same leaders who complain when the police do not react, in a timely manner, to violent crimes in their communities. They want it both ways. They feel that if they can blame the police for overreacting and blame them for not reacting it will absolve them and their communities from any responsibility. This playing two ends against the middle type of leadership has been very effective at shifting the blame. The problem is that the leadership survives and the community suffers. It should be the other way around.

When a community and its leadership do not take responsibility for their actions, they can never improve. It is like parents who blame the school administrators when their child sets fire to the school and the administrators call the police. Logical people cannot understand this type of reasoning. This type of phony leadership has become the norm in our politically correct, double-standard society. Real leaders that require those they lead to take personal responsibility for their behavior, is the secret to a family and community's success.

For many years, I have done leadership, sales, and marketing seminars for large and small businesses. When I am in my seminars, I tell my audience to only focus on the things that are within their control. For example, you have the power to control your weight, but not your height. Putting your time and energy on areas that you can control will help improve your life. Focusing on areas beyond your control will be discouraging besides being a complete waste of time. Strong effective leadership can help to influence individual and group behavior. Effective leadership is transforming a mob mentality into an effective disciplined army.

Good parents focus on the behavior of their children, not on the behavior of others outside their family. Functional families are a great model for all leaders to emulate. Functional families serve as the model that successful communities, corporations, and athletic teams follow.

When I was growing up, my father would always make me take responsibility for my actions. If I got into trouble in school, he would focus on my actions, not the teacher's reactions. He would always say to me, "I do not care what someone else did until you first tell me what you did." My father was very tough and unyielding. We had a close relationship until the day he died. I always had great respect for him and knew that he took great interest in my development.

I believe love is discipline and discipline is love. You cannot have one without the other. Parents show great love for their children when they discipline them. They are preparing their children for success in the real world.

I have made many mistakes in my life and I eventually understood my role in those mistakes. As I have gotten older, I realize that I have been a major contributor to all the good things and all the bad things that have happened in my life. Taking responsibility for your actions leads to improving your behavior. My father's principles have had a great influence in my life and I will be forever grateful.

I feel strong effective armies, communities, sports teams, and corporate leaders, etc. are most successful when they emulate the actions of a functional family. Sun Tzu was a famous Chinese general 2,500 years ago, and is quoted as having said something that I think we as parents or corporate leaders can all identify with:

"If, however, you are indulgent but unable to make your authority felt; kind-hearted, but unable to enforce your commands; and incapable, moreover, of quelling disorder: then your soldiers should be likened to spoiled children; they are useless for any practical purpose."

I see young men go to school looking like bums. Most people become a product of their environment. If you dress like a bum, you will act like a bum. Our politically correct society is permissive and discourages disciplinary confrontations. Public school officials do not feel it is their job to confront behavioral problems or unprofessional attire.

How can you possibly succeed in our competitive world without self-discipline, which includes a professional dress code? The schools are preparing our young people for a life of mediocrity. The parents of these children are most to blame because of their unwillingness to take a leadership role to confront and correct bad behavior. This was never more evident than my previous example of Joran Vander Sloot.

The PC far-left doctrine encourages parents to avoid confrontation with their children rather than strongly insert their will to solve problems. As I stated earlier, discipline is a show of love; always giving in to your children is a sign of apathy.

I believe in a school dress code. I also believe in a defined disciplined environment where students know the rules and have to conduct themselves properly or face the consequences. Those consequences would include extra homework, school projects or even expulsion. Good schools are like good companies—to run efficiently they must define and monitor a standard of excellence.

I listen in disbelief to these so-called child experts who are totally against strong discipline. They have influenced our society to the point where spanking your child is a crime. When I hear this, I tell parents to get the video or book The Miracle Worker.

It is the story of Helen Keller and her teacher Anne Sullivan. Helen Keller was deaf, dumb, and blind from early infancy. Her parents had great sympathy for their child and thought they were being good parents and showing mercy when they tolerated her out-of-control behavior. If her teacher, Anne Sullivan, did not come into her life, Helen Keller would have been institutionalized. If that had happened, it would have robbed the world of one of the most inspirational people who ever lived.

Thankfully, Anne Sullivan, through her unyielding discipline, dedication, great patience, and leadership, helped Helen Keller gain world prominence. She forcibly helped Helen Keller achieve greatness beyond her parents' limited expectations. Helen Keller eventually wrote books and could read Braille in six languages including Chinese and Greek.

Instead of being institutionalized, she became a valuable part of our society. Anne Sullivan was a great leader and the most important influence in the life of Helen Keller. Helen Keller's success was a direct reflection of Anne Sullivan's great leadership. Great leaders improve the skills and behavior of those they lead.

Correcting bad behavior is essential in personal growth. Constructive discipline is positive, not negative. When you help those around you improve, you become a valuable resource to them. To be most effective in a leadership role you need to become a role model. Do what you say and say what you do. To be a successful disciplinarian you must have great credibility. In other words, if you discipline someone's bad behavior, you must be a strong role model by never participating in that behavior.

As irresponsible as it is for parents not to discipline bad behavior, it is just as irresponsible for someone in a leadership position to excuse or defend bad behavior. When leaders avoid this important responsibility, they forfeit their effectiveness as leaders. Their family, communities, or corporation will suffer.

Michael Vick would suffer if his bad behavior was excused or, even worse, defended. It would encourage him to continue in this destructive lifestyle, which can only lead to failure and despair.

Being an effective leader takes courage, commitment, and a desire to help improve the lives of those around you. Complaining about the actions of those outside your area of influence is not only unproductive but demonstrates your lack of leadership. Bad behavior should never be excused or defended. It only leads to additional behavioral problems. When problems do arise, look first internally to solve those problems. Adopt this philosophy for you and your group: "If it is to be, it is up to me." Take responsibility for your actions and those you have influence over. This will assist you, as a leader to create a positive environment, which will ensure growth. Personal responsibility leads to success.

CHAPTER 11

Profiling: Logical or Evil

We have discussed how the far left politically correct are very idealistic. Influenced by our judicial system their conclusions many times escape logic. They have a tendency to treat every situation the same. Never seeming to recognize the severity of the situation can result in them painting all criminals and crimes with a broad brush.

I believe judicial political correctness violates the rights of the victims by over compensating the criminal. As a result many of those that commit crimes almost feel an entitlement when having to face their accusers. They are well aware that judicial manipulation prevents the truth from being heard.

As I mentioned in the preface profiling for any reason is frowned upon by our ACLU influenced judicial system. Profiling criminals is unacceptable in our politically correct society because it violates human rights. It sounds very humane and idealistic but is it logical and does it keep America safe?

I believe that most fair minded Americans believe that terrorism has created the need for profiling. Muslim fundamentalists are trying to impose their distorted religious beliefs through indiscriminate violence. We have witnessed first hand numerous acts of terror including the killing of women and children. We have recently witnessed two failed terrorists attempts one on a plane Christmas day the other was a failed car bombing in Manhattan.

Islam continues to warn the world of their diabolical plans and we have witnessed their methods. The question is when are we going to take these threats seriously? Down through the centuries there have been many terrorists that have brought death and destruction to civilization but none have been as deranged as these religious lunatics. They sacrifice their children in the name of God. Their ideology is distorted and their methods are demonic.

With all of this knowledge, profiling for reasons of race, religion, or socio-economic background is still considered politically incorrect in our politically correct society. Many in the judicial system feel it is a civil rights issue and that profiling, should never be permitted regardless of the situation. Is it a logical conclusion in today's world?

Throughout my book, I have continually described the PC protected and their idealistic view of our world. They are always ready to criticize the methods of those who protect. Their idealism is risking the lives of every American. It is very easy to judge others if you remove yourself from the equation.

Because of this idealistic approach, our judicial system is jeopardizing our safety and they seem to be oblivious. The far left, with help from the ACLU/judicial system, defend the civil rights of terrorists, even when they know their evil intentions. Islam has made it very clear that they want another 9/11 in the United States. They have terrorists living within our country who are dedicated to carrying out this threat and our judicial system is worried about profiling, wiretapping and due process. I believe civil rights should be earned and that profiling is necessary in today's volatile world. I am also convinced that the ACLU's far left idealism borders on insanity.

The reality is when groups think alike, they will be judged alike, especially if they endorse violence. When they engage in criminal activities they are judged as criminals and rightly so. This is a natural and very logical conclusion.

Islam teaches their children to hate and prepares them to kill all infidels. These religious leaders are men who preach and justify violence as a means to an end. Remember they are "religious leaders" who endorse the killing of others. I can't emphasize this point enough. While moderate Muslims remain silent on this issue and their silence is deafening. The Muslims' actions and rhetoric require them to be profiled. It's just common sense!

Muslims comprise 22% of the world's population and have infiltrated Europe and America. When polled on Islamic issues many young American Muslims agree with much of the dangerous fundamentalists' tactics and rhetoric. These tactics, less we never forget, included the destruction of the World Trade Center, which resulted in the deaths of over 3,000 innocent people. These lunatics have also been involved in planning and participating in many more, horrific crimes around the world.

Having all this information regarding Muslims, if we did not profile them, especially in airports, we should not profile anyone for any reason. If the United States adopted this position, we as a nation would be completely irresponsible. I know that when I am flying I want all Muslim passengers, to be given special attention, before being allowed to board my plane.

I do not expect the PC protected who are idealistic to agree and that is OK because they live in a dream world devoid of reality. I get very nervous if I ever agree with them on anything relating to justice. Let them in their idealistic, passive way remedy this situation. They will soon understand that the Muslim fundamentalists do not respond to peaceful compromise.

Remember, Muslim fundamentalists believe that taking the lives of non-Muslims is an honor and is instructed by their God. Until moderate Muslims, around the world, condemn these crazy fanatics with their distorted religious ideology, all Muslims should be profiled. I continue to emphasize that all Muslims have put themselves in this unfavorable position by their threats and violence or by their silence and refusal to publicly condemn these horrific criminals.

Profiling can and should be applied to Americans citizens as well as potential terrorists when the situation is warranted. If there was a convicted child molester living in your neighborhood and a child was molested in your neighborhood shouldn't they be the first interviewed? That's logical but in our far left PC world it would be considered profiling. As I said previously idealism and logic are diametrically opposed to each other especially when the ACLU intervenes.

For instance, when an automobile is vandalized or stolen, we should most likely assume that it was the work of a criminal. If so, the police should first go to high-crime areas and interview criminals that have had a history of stealing cars to try to locate and recover the stolen property. Even if the high-crime area is in the inner city and predominately black.

This does not mean the majority of black citizens are criminals but it would indicate that criminals live in that community. There is a difference. It only makes sense to investigate a crime where criminals live, right? Many of the far left PC would say wrong. They would contend that any neighborhood is just as likely to have criminals who commit these crimes, even when there is no history of crime in that neighborhood. It makes little sense but it makes them feel very liberal.

Profiling a high-crime area when a crime is committed is discouraged by the far-left politically correct. I do not know if they are incredibly naive or purposely try to distort the truth to meet their crazy agenda. High-crime areas are where criminals live. That is why they are high-crime areas.

Let me give you an actual situation that happened to a member of my family. One night, while my cousin and his wife were sleeping, someone broke into their car and stole it. My cousin felt violated because he lives in a nice area with very little crime.

They immediately called the police and gave them a detailed report. After three days of waiting and anguishing over the loss of their car with no response, they decided to take matters in their own hands and go to a high-crime area not far from their home to investigate. It was little more than a hope and a prayer but it was better than waiting.

They did not look at more affluent low-crime areas closer to their home for their car. They went first to an area where most crimes were committed. In other words, they were engaged in profiling. Guess what, they found their car. It was in a vacant lot in a very dangerous, high-crime neighborhood. My cousin had a set of keys, jumped into his stolen car, and sped away.

When he got home, he called and met with the police

to explain the sequence of events that led to the discovery and securing of his car. The police officer was happy that they recovered the car but thought he and his wife took a big chance even entering that neighborhood. My cousin wondered why the police did not look there first. The car was in an empty lot that was visible from the main street and still had its license plates. The car was in plain view of passing traffic.

If he and his wife were able to find his car without any problem, why were the police unable to do so?

Could it be that the police are discouraged from entering these areas for fear of being accused of profiling? The politically correct would still argue that the more affluent areas are as likely to have stolen property as the high crime areas no matter what the evidence indicated. That type of reasoning is ridiculous, but sounds more humane and conforms to their human rights agenda. To me, that kind of reasoning is like trying to put a round peg in a square hole. It is denying that a problem exists, even when it is undeniable.

Putting your head in the sand and not addressing real-world problems with real-world solutions only makes our communities and world less safe. There are violent criminals, including terrorists, who are waiting to attack unsuspecting victims. Not addressing the problem does not alleviate the problem. It just makes it worse. What makes the situation even more dangerous is that our judicial system, with influence from the politically correct out-of-control ACLU, tries to imply that all people, no matter how violent and corrupt, share the same history, none better and none worse.

This is how the PC protected view the world, and it puts

all of us in jeopardy. To me, you have to prove your worth through your actions. **If my cousin went to the low-crime areas to look for his car, he would have been politically correct. He just would not have found his car.**

CHAPTER 12

Permissiveness, PC Style

Leadership takes courage. Having authority over the welfare of a group is an important role and not for the faint hearted. Effective leadership defines expectations and monitors results. Strong leaders rarely engage in permissiveness. They command respect and demand performance. Successful parents, coaches, and corporate management have one thing in common— they improve the lives of those they lead. That is what defines their success. They do not blame others for their failures and they create a standard of excellence that all must meet. My definition of permissiveness is to be afraid or unwilling to confront bad or criminal behavior. A society that becomes overly permissive is in danger of creating anarchy.

We have become a very politically correct permissive society, and it is killing us. We make excuses and tolerate all kinds of bad behavior. We allow so called experts to tell society how flawed our traditional Judeo-Christian values are. Child psychologists tell us to never spank our children and to overlook out-of-control behavior rather than confronting our children and forcing them to do what is right at an early age. We are raising a generation of spoiled children without discipline or the fear of reprisal. We are not preparing them for the real world.

Many parents do not understand their role. They want to be their child's friend instead of being the child's mentor.

They have allowed their children to take control of their home. **When children are in charge of the home, it is a dysfunctional family.**

Charles Barkley, the NBA Hall of Fame basketball player, once said that it was not his job to be a role model, and I agree with him. It is the parents' job to be role models to their children—not some celebrity athlete. I think Charles Barkley was on the money; however, he was criticized for his comments. Parents want people outside their home to do their job.

Our society promotes and encourages this type of nonsense. It is legal for a thirteen-year-old girl who wants an abortion, to have it without parental permission. If that same thirteen-year-old breaks a window, her parents must be notified and are responsible for the damage. An abortion could scar that child for life but it is not important enough to involve the parents. What politically correct BS.

Our schools have become so politically correct that students are not learning. We rank twenty-fifth out of the twenty-six industrialized countries in the world in education. In fact, schools have become places where our children are negatively influenced. It is more important to have an inadequate curriculum with a politically correct agenda than to focus on successfully teaching the students. It is also politically correct to cater to the unproductive troublemakers than it is to focus on the high achievers.

Politically correct schools have adopted the squeaky-wheel method of teaching. That is, the more trouble students cause the more positive attention they will receive. Instead of blaming the child for their disturbances, the PCs blame society. Permissiveness is an important element of this politically correct garbage. To reprimand is cruel—to blame others is politically correct.

This ideology is created and supported by the judicial system and that is why many liberal judges hand down such lenient sentences to criminals who commit violent acts. The problem is that it has the opposite affect; it is kind to the criminal and cruel to society. We discussed in the Bad Behavior chapter the terrible consequences this can lead to.

As I said, a society that becomes overly permissive is in danger of creating anarchy. New Orleans was and is an example of a city in anarchy because of their permissive, far-left judicial system. In 2006, there were over 130 murders committed with only one conviction. The gangsters, thugs and murderers' civil rights have precedence over the innocent. What far-left permissive BS.

This type of permissiveness was also evident in Boulder, Colorado when high school officials staged a mandatory assembly featuring speakers who approved of drug use, same-sex relationships, and sexual activity without condoms. You might as well have had a student seminar on how to commit suicide. When school officials were confronted with their choice of speakers and the content, they defended their position. Dr. George Garcia, Boulder school superintendent, would not condemn these speakers. Maybe he does not realize that unprotected sex and indiscriminate drug use can lead to AIDS.

How can this information benefit students? What school officials can be assured of is that they will be vigorously defended by the far-left politically correct ACLU because it is in line with their distorted secular ideology. The ACLU rejects anything that is traditional.

What would have been the reaction if the school decided to feature a group of speakers encouraging students to refrain from sex and drug use, live clean lives, and even attend their places of worship? School officials would think this was outrageous — especially the religious aspect. Separation of church and state, you know.

In our secular wrong-is-right society permissiveness is encouraged and defended, while traditional behavior is attacked and ridiculed. The far-left PCs believe that a society that is not permissive is oppressive. Requiring permission from those in authority is considered an infringement of an individual's civil rights, especially when the authority figures believe in traditional values.

Another example of this is the Boy Scouts. The PCs hate the Boy Scouts and everything they stand for. The Scouts do not allow homo sexual leaders and they preach a message of abstinence, clean living, and religious awareness. This is a hateful message to the permissive PCs. If this type of reasoning is not an indication that many of the far-left politically correct are insane with a distorted agenda, I don't know what is!

A fifth-grade class in a southwest Florida middle school reportedly listed a book entitled Life is Funny by E.R. Frank as mandatory reading. The book contains profanity, pornography, etc. Reading this book can only help to damage and confuse children. Children require guidance from responsible adults. For a book like this to be mandatory reading in the fifth grade demonstrates that the far-left politically correct have taken over our educational system. The educators who have allowed them to do this are irresponsible.

Parents of these children, by remaining silent, have allowed a politically correct agenda to become acceptable. Not challenging this secular distortion is also irresponsible. The far-left elite have intimidated the parents who question this nonsense. They are accused of being old-fashion and ignorant.

We see children who dress like degenerates with their pants down around their rear ends with their underwear showing. Many pierce their bodies and have tattoos, while parents and school officials remain silent. There is no adult guidance or supervision, and our society is paying the price. You might as well not have parents or adults running the schools if they allow children to act like this.

We see sex offenders, who are habitual criminals, given an insignificant punishment for horrific crimes against children. Our judicial system will not take the lead and keep us safe. They have given into the politically correct value system, which is devoid of traditional values, as well as common sense. Our permissive society is putting everyone at risk. When weak immoral leadership in our society is leading to our demise, we should rebel and refuse to accept it.

We live in a democratic society where the majority, is supposed to rule. We must have the courage to stand for what is right. We are allowing a small group of far-left secular elitists dictate our values. They are devoid of values yet are trying to determine and establish a value system for the rest of us. Adopting their distorted value system is like replacing Mother Theresa's core values and sensitivity with Keith Olbermann's.

Everything starts with the family. We must be role models

for our children, always aware of their surroundings, teaching them right from wrong, and disciplining whenever necessary. Parents must never be left out of the decision-making process concerning their children in or out of school. We must insist that our schools teach values as well as math and science. We must also insist that our laws are fair and logical. School administrators and politicians work for us and we should hold them accountable for their actions.

We should vigorously oppose far-left groups like the ACLU and their distorted secular agenda. If our political leaders understand the majority of society is against secular groups like the ACLU, they will start to respond or we can vote them out. Just because a small vocal group aggressively defends this permissiveness, that does not make it right.

When I evaluate what the ACLU has stood for over the years, I know that their values do not reflect the Judeo-Christian values that this country was built on. The ACLU says that we cannot pray in our schools, yet we should remain silent and allow the immoral garbage that attacks our traditional values to exist. If our values are righteous, we should defend them or we will lose them. Permissiveness is a huge part of the PC agenda. The more permissive society becomes, the easier it will be for them to carry out their distorted twisted ideology.

CHAPTER 13

Second Amendment

Our Constitution is being manipulated by the far left politically correct and the judicial system. In fact it is difficult to tell the two apart. If they cannot redefine its meaning to serve their agenda they will change the actual wording to suit their purposes. Their far left activism is undermining our Constitution and will eventually destroy our country. President John Adams said "remember democracy never lasts long. It soon wastes, exhausts, and murders itself. There never was a democracy yet that did not commit suicide."

It amazes me how intelligent and visionary our founding fathers were. They wrote a document that has stood the test of time. The second amendment to the Constitution gives Americans the right to bear arms and it is now under attack.

I have great empathy for all those who want to end violence in our country. They are very passionate and many believe that gun control will end indiscriminate killings. Where I disagree with them is that their definition of gun control is the banning of all firearms. I believe that taking guns away from law-abiding citizens will put our society in more danger. Guns are not the problem, our judicial system is.

I believe the only way we can ensure the safety of our citizens in through court reform, not gun control. Our failed judicial system with its many procedures put us in much more danger than honest citizens owning guns. Putting criminals back on our streets through procedural technicalities forces society to purchase guns.

The United States Constitution is the supreme law of our land. It was adopted on September 17, 1787, by the Constitutional Convention in Philadelphia. The United States Bill of Rights includes the ten amendments added to the Constitution in 1791. The second amendment gives all citizens the right to bear arms. It states "A well regulated militia, being necessary to the security of a free state, the right of the people to keep and bear arms, shall not be infringed." This has come under great scrutiny by anti-gun activists. The activists and the National Rifle Association (NRA) are in great conflict over this issue. I understand and have empathy for both sides of this issue.

From a protected activist point of view, they can say that violent criminals using firearms commit most of the murders in our country and I am sure they are correct. They feel if all firearms were confiscated our country would be safer. Many feel that there is no need for anyone to own assault weapons, armor piercing bullets and concealed weapons (handguns).

The question we need to ask is, if all the firearms in the United States were seized today, would that have an affect on our countries murder rate? I believe it would initially result in a huge decline in murders.

So why is there not a public outcry to make this happen? Wouldn't we all be safer? No, and here is why. Let us look at this situation from a realistic point of view. Violent criminals commit violent crimes. Law abiding citizens do not. Criminals will always be able to get guns. It is like drugs. Drugs have always been outlawed in the United States but that has never kept the drug dealers from getting drugs. Drug dealers can get all the drugs they will ever need; in fact, **it is more difficult for some in our society to get their prescription filled than for drug dealers to get drugs.**

It would be the same with guns. I have never been concerned with honest people in our society owning guns. They do not commit crimes. They are not a threat to society. That said I do think that assault weapons and armor piercing bullets are an abuse of the second amendment. All other firearms that are in the hands of honest people are fine with me. In fact, in our violent society with its judicial loop holes I encourage you to do what is necessary to keep your family safe.

I refer to the judicial system because the Fourth Amendment is also part of the dilemma. It guards against searches, arrests and seizures of property without specific warrant or a "probable cause" to believe a crime has been committed. Some rights to privacy have been inferred from this amendment and others by the Supreme Court. Our judicial system and loophole savvy lawyers can have a field day with this amendment and when they do society suffers, especially the "probable cause" part.

Continuing to examine the problem from a realistic point of view, I conclude that our judicial system is the reason for this controversy. Criminals are released back into society because the criminal defense attorneys manipulate our justice system or lenient judge's hand down inappropriate sentences for horrific crimes. After their release, these habitual criminals continue to inflict great personal injury on their unsuspecting victims. Instead of the judicial system recognizing the problem and tightening the procedures that caused the problem, they defend them.

It becomes a catch twenty-two. The criminals are the reason for the public feeling the need to carry concealed weapons for protection and the judicial system was the reason for the criminals being released. Either way gun control will not fix the problem.

Yet many criminal defense attorneys are adamant about the need for gun control. I think they refuse to believe that they are a big part of the problem. Until we can come up with a solution to this dilemma, I think innocent gun owners need to keep their guns and defend their Constitutional rights.

I am ignorant enough to believe that our founding fathers created documents, the Constitution and the Bill of Rights and designed them to protect the innocent. Instead, they are being manipulated by the judicial system to benefit the guilty. It is a double whammy as I stated earlier, the criminal violates society and their lawyers manipulate our Constitution to help them avoid prosecution.

Many criminals that commit violent crimes are habitual predators and are not easily, rehabilitated. Yet they are put back into society by our failed court system to continue their assaults. The judicial system is the problem yet they continue to blame gun ownership for the problem. An unarmed society becomes easy prey. If law-abiding citizens happen to encounter these predators in their homes, how do they protect themselves and their families without access to a firearm?

Let me give you a tragic situation that happened near Ithaca, New York, many years ago to a family of four. Two predators entered their home tied the entire family up raped the mother and daughter and then executed all of them. One of the predators was a habitual criminal with a very violent past and yet was free to destroy more lives. In life there may be times you are faced with a life and death situation. When this happens it is better to be prepared than sorry.

Another concern when you disarm a society is the threat of a possible terrorist attack. Ever since 9/11, I have wondered when another terrorist attack will happen. Our borders are not secure and we have an enemy who is focused on destroying us. In my opinion, another terrorist attack is eminent. We as citizens may need to protect ourselves from criminals or terrorists if the police are unable to do so.

The need to be able to protect yourself was never more evident than after hurricane Katrina slammed into New Orleans. The result was complete devastation and confusion. Gangs and thugs roamed the streets heavily armed. They were looting and intimidating the citizens of New Orleans. There were not enough police to handle the situation and as a result, it created anarchy. The criminal element was in control of various areas of the city. Murders increased and law and order has not been fully restored.

How would you like to be in that situation and unable to defend yourself or your family? I am sure it would be very frightening and if the anti-gun protected experienced that situation, perhaps it would affect their thinking on this issue. If the police cannot protect you and your family and the courts are in disarray, you had better find a way to protect yourself. It becomes a matter of survival.

The United States is a very violent country and much of the problem has to be attributed to our failed judicial system, as I stated earlier. Gang activity is at an all time high threatening our citizens. We have illegal immigrants crossing our borders in great numbers. Many of the illegal are bringing drugs into our country. Our leaders in Washington are afraid of their own shadows when it comes to confronting activist groups. Terrorist's cells are operating in our country with evil intentions for our citizens.

Feeling the need to protect yourself is a basic instinct especially during these volatile times. Feeling the need to have a gun in the home is an individual's right, protected by our Constitution and should not be redefined by the government. Besides, the vast majority of gun owners are outdoor sports enthusiasts who engage in hunting, target practice, etc. Gun owners are not the problem, criminals are.

Do not try to force gun legislation on society.

Instead, let us all demand court reform and work to make our streets safer. When we do, there will be less need for society to acquire guns. Take away the need for society to own guns by doing the following:

1. Make sure that everyone who applies for a gun permit is given a complete background check that gives previous criminal and mental history. There should be a set waiting period for everyone who applies with no exceptions. This will help to keep the criminal element out.

2. Close our borders to all illegal aliens and deport the criminal element. Find a way for illegal immigrants who are not criminals to gain citizenship. This will also help stop the drain in our economy.

3. Redesign our judicial system to benefit the victim and penalize the criminal by closing judicial loopholes and imposing mandatory sentencing. Take the authority away

from lenient judges and crafty defense attorneys.

4. Then make a concerted effort to disband the gangs that victimize people throughout our country, similar to what the FBI did to the Mafia. We need to find a way to successfully rehabilitate these gang members, so they can become functional members of society. I know this will be very difficult to do but something has to be done to eliminate the threat these gangs pose to society.

When our streets are safe and our justice system becomes just, society will find little reason to own a gun other than for sport. It is our constitutional right to carry guns. Law-abiding citizens who carry guns are not the problem because they do not commit crimes. The manipulation of our judicial system is the problem. Crimes are committed by criminals and not by innocent gun owners. Do not believe the far-left politically correct propaganda.

CHAPTER 14

Police Abused

In this chapter I am going to continue to expose those who I believe are putting society at risk. I know that I have been very critical of our judges, lawyers and politicians. I feel that they absolve themselves of any responsibility concerning our nations increase in crime.

I do not know whether to laugh or cry when I hear criminal defense attorneys play the police abuse card. That is like cats accusing mice of not playing fair. It is manipulation and deception at its lowest level. Criminal defense attorneys who prevent the truth from being introduced if it indicates their clients' guilt and passing judgment on the police for using force to apprehend a criminal are shameful. Attorneys can misrepresent the truth while condemning police officers for defending themselves when confronting criminals.

Being in law enforcement is an honorable career. The vast majority of police officers are well-trained professionals dedicated to doing their best at keeping our homes and streets safe. Whenever we feel threatened, we call them to protect us. Police officers are truly servants of the people.

Today's police officers have to be a combination of politician and foot soldier. Politicians need to cover their tracks and use diplomacy in their approach, always being aware of the political/judicial ramifications of their actions. Foot soldiers have to be ready for battle at a moment's notice, risking their lives in the defense of others. They have to do battle with the criminals on the streets as well as justify their actions to the defense attorneys. It is a dangerous and thankless job. They truly are society's protectors.

Our judicial system has made it increasingly difficult to be an effective police officer. The judicial procedural system has become very complicated. The system errs on the side of those who commit crimes, not with the victim, and certainly not with the police. Police officers are viewed under a magnifying glass when they make an arrest. No matter how horrific the crime or the criminal, police must justify their actions.

If they apprehend a murderer committing a crime, they can still be criticized for being overly aggressive in making the arrest. Police brutality is a common tactic used by criminal defense attorneys.

Police officers have resorted to using cameras to record their arrests to guard against police brutality charges, and sometimes those cameras can be used against them. Because of the use of these cameras, we have all been able to witness police cars speeding after suspected criminals and police risking their lives trying to apprehend those criminals.

The car chases are so fast and the pursuits are so dangerous it can get my adrenalin pumping and I am in the safety of my home. Imagine what it must be like in real life. The criminals commit a crime, flee the scene in a speeding car, jeopardizing the lives of everyone in their path, and it is the police who are often criticized for using excessive force when they apprehend the criminals.

Criminal defense attorneys often focus on the police and their arrest methods. It can be an effective way to divert attention away from the criminals they defend. It is so easy to place blame on the police from the safety of a courtroom where you do not have to actually engage in the hand-to-hand combat and make lifesaving decisions under extreme pressure.

I believe criminals resisting arrest should be treated with as much force as it takes to arrest them. There should be no such thing as excessive force with criminals who are trying to resist arrest especially when they have destroyed innocent lives. It is idealistic to think otherwise, especially, as I said, when you never have to personally engage them.

There is an old saying that the definition of a conservative is a liberal who has been mugged. When you face a life-and-death situation, you have a completely different thought process. Survival is a wonderful reality check.

I recommend that we redirect our focus. Let us start looking at criminal defense attorneys who will use every method possible to put the criminals they defend back on the street. These criminals can be rapists, murderers, and child molesters; it does not matter. They can be habitual criminals and yet authorities release them back into society without regard for the safety of our communities. Let us start holding these criminal defense attorneys and judges liable for the crimes committed by the criminals they helped release.

Our thought process is backward. We second-guess the police officers, society's protectors who risk their lives, and question their arrest procedures when apprehending dangerous criminals; we say nothing about the tactics criminal defense attorneys use. Who is keeping us safe the police or the defense attorneys? Next time someone is attacking you, call a criminal defense attorney. But if you do, remember he or she may work very hard to get your attacker off through a technicality. When authorities put violent criminals back on the street, the police as well as the public are in jeopardy.

Most criminal defense attorneys are proud of what they do. They feel they are doing a service to society when they help their clients avoid punishment for their crimes. They do not care how many crimes the criminals they are defending committed and how their release will affect society. They take pride in their ability to use the system and all the technicalities to their advantage.

Are they doing society or their own pocketbooks a service? When it is a high-profile crime, the good criminal defense attorneys will line up to offer their services. The exposure on how they manipulate the system will help them gain more recognition and money. I have no idea how they sleep at night knowing they just put a dangerous felon back on the street to violate additional innocent people.

Defense attorneys use procedural manipulation and deception to put criminals back on the street, which creates additional innocent victims. Police officers risk their lives to keep our communities safe by arresting criminals. Many criminals become habitual offenders throughout our system. Yet most criminal defense attorneys are highly regarded among their highly paid peers and they vehemently defend the system, while considering police officers a necessary evil.

I believe that police officers are the ones being abused, either by criminals, who jeopardize officers' lives by resisting arrest, or by the criminals' attorney, who try to make the arresting officers the issue, not the criminals. I have a great regard for most police officers and applaud their job performance. We ask them to risk their lives to keep us safe and they do that every day. Most of us would be shocked if we spent a day with them while they are performing their duties.

As citizens, we should demand court reform.

Currently the lawyers manipulate the laws for their own benefit. When criminal defense attorneys prevent juries from hearing truthful evidence, they call it proper procedure—I call it lying. A rat by any other name is still a rat. They have created a system that allows them to cheat legally.

To change this vicious self-serving cycle, I recommend we choose a panel that includes high ranking police officers and others, not just lawyers, to determine a logical set of judicial procedural rules that will benefit society. Where the innocent victim will find justice, and the criminals and their attorneys will be less likely to manipulate the system. So many lives have been lost because of our failed justice system. The wealthier the criminal defense attorneys become, the more unsafe society is.

We should also have mandatory sentencing. We currently leave it up to judges to determine the punishment to fit the crime. The criminal element is encouraged when a judge hands down lenient sentences.

Two examples of judges more interested in the criminal's rights than the victim's rights are first, the case of the judge who let nine youths who gang raped a 10 year old girl in Cape York walk, without any jail time . Judge Sarah Bradley determined that the 10 year girl probably agreed to have sex with the gang. A second case involved a 13 year old deaf boy who was molested. Instead of his attacker being incarcerated, he was given a suspended sentence. Judge Michael Kelly determined that the handicapped youth was merely engaging in an adolescent experimentation. I wonder if these judges would be as forgiving if their family members were the victims.

Judges that render these horrific decisions are encouraging criminal behavior. The defense attorney's who engage in, what I refer to as procedural misconduct, by allowing such criminals to escape justice, are also at fault. Police abuse, is publicized and criticized.

The judicial system is never confronted with "procedural abuse". We as citizens have allowed the judges and lawyers to develop their "unfair" system and then let them evaluate it.

When you question judges or lawyers on the failures of our system, they all reply the same way. They say it is the best system in the world. Does that mean the system is good and does not need changing or does that mean the system is beneficial to them? I think it is the latter.

Do police officers make mistakes? Every day and should be held accountable for their mistakes. Do police officers benefit when they make mistakes? Rarely, and their paychecks prove it. Do criminal defense attorneys benefit when they help a guilty criminal avoid prosecution? Yes and they are rarely held accountable and their paychecks prove it too.

The difference is that when police officers make a mistake, it often happens in the heat of battle when they are engaged in a struggle for survival. We should cut them some slack, because we have been excusing criminal defense attorneys' tactics for years. Police are overworked and under appreciated in our society.

If we want a free and open society where we as citizens can feel safe, we should encourage well trained police officers to perform their duties, not prevent them from doing so. Many times the technicalities in our judicial system prevent police officers from doing their job.

Police abuse, there is definitely some. Criminal abuse, of police officers definitely. Societal abuse, by criminal defense attorneys, most definitely!

Police officers are the protectors risking their lives to defend society. Criminal defense attorneys are the protected who help increase the risk to society. When you are an innocent victim and need help, call the police. Most are dedicated professionals ready and willing to help. Our failed justice system has become a politically correct distortion of truth.

CHAPTER 15

Truth vs. Myth

We have talked about "putting the round peg in the square hole" mentality. If you have a hammer and are dedicated to making it fit, it will. Forcing a myth to become truth is similar. An example of this is when the far left try to dress up Fidel Castro to make him look like a wonderful leader of the people—they are demonstrating the round-peg-square-hole mentality. It sounds great and the more you say it, the more you start to believe it. The truth of the situation tells a completely different story. That is why the truth is usually omitted when it involves far-left ideology. The majority of it is far-left propaganda and it is complete BS. That is why I wrote this book, to expose this ideology.

We as a society have been so inundated with the politically correct agenda it is hard to determine fact from fiction. The PCs have told us that our system of government is oppressive, our military is barbaric, our Judeo-Christian traditional values are exclusionary, and we are the most racist country in the world. The far left seem to hate America and everything we stand for. Let us separate truth from myth.

Our democracy has many flaws and is not perfect. Money, greed, and power by our political parties and some major corporations have gotten many of us to lose confidence in America's integrity. We as a nation are not perfect, but we are certainly not oppressive to our people. We take very seriously our Constitution and Bill of Rights, and they help to ensure our freedom. Personal freedom is America's greatest weapon against oppression.

We allow freedom of speech even when our citizens attack our own government. We can call the president of our country terrible, vile names without fear of reprisal. We can peacefully demonstrate in the streets, protesting our government's policies, without fear of incarceration. We can go to foreign countries and say disparaging things about America and our form of government without the fear of criminal repercussions when we return. People like Harry Belafonte and Danny Glover do it all the time and have never had to worry about the consequences.

If you think our government is oppressive, try to commit these acts of disobedience in Cuba. Many Cubans have risked their lives to escape from Cuba because of the oppression they face, yet these silly entertainers and athletes embrace Castro and continue to hold him in high regard as a liberator (Kaepernick) instead of the tyrant that he was. The politically correct far left love Castro and hate America, especially former President Bush and now President Trump.

To compare apples with apples, Americans who feel oppressed should go to Cuba, become citizens, and when they think the Cuban government is out of line with the people, they should demonstrate against the government. If they do this, they will have a much greater appreciation of America. They will also find out if the Cuban prisons are as inhumane as rumored.

Fidel Castro was one of the world's greatest tyrants and did not tolerate political dissent. He was the great oppressor and punished all those who challenged his authority. That is why Cubans risked their lives to cross shark-infested waters to gain political asylum in the United States. If the United States is so bad, why does everyone want to come here? And if Cuba is so good, why do so many people want to leave? These are logical questions that deserve logical answers not some far left spin.

The far left is continually criticizing our military for being barbaric in our treatment of prisoners. The PCs point to our prison in Guantanamo Bay and try to demonstrate how inhumane we are with captured terrorists. They are totally against torture of any kind for any reason. The PCs believe that even if we obtained valuable information through torture to prevent another 9/11, we should never engage in torture. The idealistic approach is to treat these lunatic terrorists with dignity and respect. To them it is inhumane to torture, and to me it is protecting society.

As I mentioned before, I keep referring to two types of people in the USA—those who protect and those who are protected. The protectors do the hard work and keep us safe. Police officers, firefighters and military service personnel put their lives on the line every day so the protected are free to live and protest. Many times the protected take for granted the sacrifices of their protectors and as a result do not appreciate their efforts. The far-left PC protected have no idea what war is all about and therefore have a completely different outlook on what it takes to ensure freedom.

If information gathered through water torture will help ensure our freedom, I am in complete favor of it. The far-left PC protected, do not understand the brutality of the Islamic enemy we face. They do not have to, because they will never put their lives on the line to engage them. The PC protected can criticize our military because they have kept us safe and free. The ACLU, our enemy's greatest ally, defends our enemies from their secure offices, never having to put their lives on the line. What would our country be without our protectors in this hostile world?

Our country's values have been built on Judeo-Christian principles. These principles are moral and just. They have been our moral foundation and have helped America become great. America has attracted immigrants from all over the world who were seeking freedom. Countries like Cuba and Venezuela do not have to worry about a large influx of immigrants trying to get into their countries. I keep asking when is the last time you heard of American's risking their lives in shark infested waters to gain asylum in Cuba. The answer to this question is never. Normal intelligent people do not want to settle in a dictatorship.

To compare any country's values and freedoms, especially Cuba and Venezuela, with the United States, is ludicrous. The biggest worry I have is losing our traditional values in favor of a politically correct secular culture because it is devoid of traditional morals and ethics.

We have taken prayer out of our schools and replaced it with far-left secular garbage. Our students are encouraged to experiment with sex and drugs at a young age. Sound ethics and morals are being replaced with this immoral nonsense. Our family values, which made our country great, are now, considered passé. The far-left politically correct, who do not share these values, are trying to replace them with their distorted value system. President John Adams (1797-1801) said "Our Constitution was made only for a moral and religious people. It is wholly inadequate to the government of any other."

Judeo-Christian values and principles are Bible based and God inspired and the foundation upon which our country was built. The PC values are secular based and man inspired. We can see the difference in the PC justice system's leniency toward the criminal, to the exclusion of the victim. Removing God's influence from our lives and replacing it with confusion causes upheaval. If we allow this to continue, we will become a haven of depravity. Remember those words from a founding father, to paraphrase, those without morals and religion will determine our Constitution to be inadequate.

As I have referred to in previous chapters racism is another area where the far-left PC gang criticizes America as cruel and intolerant. The white establishment has always been criticized and accused of being racist by everyone from the far-left university professors to black and white activist groups. People like Al Sharpton and Jesse Jackson have made a very lucrative career out of doing so. The PCs always point to the mistreatment of black Americans, especially when it comes to the history of African slavery. Let's review that history.

Members of African tribes sold slaves into captivity. The slave trade was a huge business; slavery is thousands of years old and universal in its scope. Africans themselves owned slaves as well as Arabs, Asians, and Europeans. Slavery was not solely a white disgrace; it was a world disgrace.

As a sidebar, when doing my research on slavery, I found that the end of slavery did not end racism as I alluded to earlier. Many Americans were guilty of racism against blacks well after the Emancipation Proclamation ended slavery. I do not want to minimize that detail in this chapter.

In fact, it was the early 1960s in the United States before

legislation was passed to ensure the end of segregation in our Southern states. That is an established fact and cannot be disputed. But, slavery and racism are two completely different issues and should be examined separately.

Slavery is the domination and ownership of an individual or group by another individual or group. It causes servitude and enslavement and is performed against the individual's will. Racism is discrimination against any individual or group solely based on race and skin color. Slavery is domination and racism is discrimination.

Both are unacceptable in a free and democratic society. As previously discussed legislation to eradicate slavery in America was enacted in 1865. It proclaimed that it was against the law to own slaves. It took much longer to end slavery around the world, especially in Muslim and Asian countries.

There is also legislation to prevent racism in the workplace and in the housing market, etc., but there is no legislation that can change the minds of ignorant racist people, only behavior can. When most people have a chance to interact with different ethnic groups, they realize that we are all basically the same, especially over time as people evolve and become more sophisticated.

Racism comes about by ignorance and fear; understanding and tolerance will usually eradicate racism with the majority of educated people. Racism will never end for those, black or white who love to hate.

Racism is embraced and encouraged by those who need to blame others for their failures. One thing that I know for sure is that racists will always accuse others of racism. Some groups are encouraged to use racism whenever they are denied access.

They never look internally; they always look at and condemn those around them. That is what they do and they do it well. It is also a good way to identify bigots for who they really are.

Many black Americans have converted to the Muslim faith to disassociate themselves from the "white European slave owner." They blame Europeans for the perpetration of slavery, and that is a myth. The truth is that Europeans, most notably the English, forcibly put an end to worldwide slavery. I said forcibly because that is what it took to end slavery around the world, especially in the Muslim countries.

The English had the largest empire in the world.

Almost one-forth of the world was part of that empire. The Royal Navy, the strongest and most advanced navy in the world, greatly influenced the eventual end of slavery.

The Muslims, on the other hand, were totally against ending slavery and had to be forced by the Europeans to do so. Slavery in the Arab countries was still going strong well after it ended in the United States. What made this effort by the English so honorable was that it was not profitable to end slavery. In other words, they ended slavery because it was inhumane even though it was profitable.

Abraham Lincoln wrote the Emancipation Proclamation, which eventually freed the slaves. It was white Americans (European immigrants), that ended slavery in our country and many have worked hard at trying to end racism. Islam, on the other hand, did not want slavery to end and engaged in this evil practice well after the Emancipation Proclamation.

I know many Muslim leaders may dispute it, but it is true that the Europeans stopped slavery and it is a myth to excuse the Muslims. I am totally convinced that if the Europeans did not force an end to slavery it would still be practiced around the world today especially in the Arab countries.

Many have allowed the European slavery myth to become truth because it fits into their far-left agenda. As I stated previously, guilt can be a very effective strategy in trying to achieve a double standard.

Black Americans that have converted to Islam do not realize how deeply rooted Islam was in slavery. In fact many still treat their women as slaves. Islam is awarded a pass on the slavery issue because of the lack of knowledge on this issue and not because of their lack of participation. Slavery, in America, existed approximately three hundred years (early 1500's-1865) and thousands of years worldwide.

We are the home of the brave and the land of the free. There is not another country in the world with our freedoms. Our government, with all its flaws, is of the people and for the people. Our traditional values are based on a higher authority, and achieving those values is what all good Americans strive for.

Myths can become truth when the misinformed aggressively embrace them. When you see members of our society embrace a tyrant or dictator as a hero, do not be fooled. It is the misinformed far-left PCs who are wrong, not the majority of our society. When our military is accused of being barbaric and our enemies' tactics are justified, consider the distorted source of the information. When our traditional values are challenged by the far left, understand their secular purpose and ideology. When Americans are accused of being intolerant, remember it is most often the most intolerant that are the accusers.

My criteria for truth, is I always know that I am on the right track when I disagree with the far left secular ideology. I will start to question my principles and values if I ever start to agree with them.

CHAPTER 16

Christmas

I continue to discuss subjects that I feel are most controversial. I am trying to challenge the politically correct by discussing traditional values that have made America great. Each chapter of my book is intended to stimulate thought and provide my readers with the courage to voice and defend their traditions without intimidation. The celebration of Christmas is another tradition that is being attacked.

In the United States, approximately 80% of Americans are Christian and celebrate Christmas, the birth of Jesus Christ. It is a very religious holiday among Christians. We buy hundreds of millions of dollars in gifts and food in celebration of this holiday every year. Christmas and gift giving is a huge economic stimulant to the success of our economy.

Recently Christmas has come under attack by the secular minority who challenge the religious aspects of this holiday. Many of them feel the mere mention of Christmas is offensive to those who are not Christian. They are the far-left politically correct seculars who are devoid of religious beliefs and resent those of us who do have faith. Instead of a live and let live mentality, they continually try to impose their non-religious values on the rest of us. They are so secular that any mention of religion is offense to them, even though our country was built on God's principles. Thomas Jefferson said "I tremble for my country when I reflect that God is just; that his justice cannot sleep forever."

When looking into this issue I was as interested in examining why they were trying to attack Christians and our holiday, as much as I was interested in the attack itself, and I have a theory. Most seculars are far left and very liberal. Most evangelical Christians are far right and conservative. In previous elections the far right was very organized and supported a platform based on traditional Judeo-Christian values. The Christian vote was critical in the election and reelection of George W. Bush and Donald Trump. Since the far left hate former President Bush and Trump with a passion, they blame the evangelicals for their presidency. They are now in a hateful frenzy and will do anything to try to eliminate the threat of the far right Christian collation and take great enjoyment in attacking their values. The problem with this strategy is that when you attack a group's religious values, you often re energize that group. It is only a theory but I think their hatred is as much about politics as it is about religion.

That said, in America the majority rules, or at least it is suppose to. The majority of Americans are Christian yet the far-left secular minority is attacking Christians because of their religious and political beliefs. The far left are a liberal minority that the equally radical ACLU supports.

The far left are never concerned with the Muslim or Jewish holidays even though both are very religious groups that openly celebrate their traditions. That is why I concluded that the far left are politically as well as religiously motivated in their attacks on Christians. The fact that most of these seculars are void of traditional and religious values makes their assault that much more vicious because they will say or do anything to make their point.

The far left's attacks are not against any other religion

except Christianity. The far-left seculars hate and feel threatened by Christians because their secular values are so diametrically opposed to Christian values. They seem to support any organization or group that is anti-Christian.

The ACLU is the far-left seculars, biggest supporter because they share the same values, which amount to no religious values at all. Christians are a threat because of their conservative political beliefs, their traditional values and their strong faith in God. Far-left seculars are liberal, anti-traditional values, and anti-God.

As a result, Christmas parties have been changed to holiday parties. Christmas vacations have been changed to holiday vacations. The manger has been outlawed in many cities, even when Jewish and Muslim religious symbols are allowed. Both groups are permitted to display their religious symbols in schools and shopping centers while Christians, who make up 80% of the population, are rarely allowed to display a manger. Both of these religious groups, as I said, are a minority in this country, yet their holidays are given more respect than Christmas.

This has caused great concern among many Christians. We are trying to fight a far-left minority in a society that is becoming increasingly secular. The seculars are trying to make Christians feel guilty for their traditional values and religious beliefs. As a Christian, these attacks have actually strengthened my resolve and increased my faith. In fact, I think the attack on Christmas, should be a wake-up call to all Christians, and viewed as a positive, not a negative. It forces us to reevaluate our focus of gift giving as well as our commitment to the true meaning of our holy day.

Christians are the reason Christmas is so commercialized. Christians spend huge amounts of money celebrating the birth of Jesus Christ. The Christmas season is the single biggest economic stimulant to the growth of our economy, yet even some merchants, trying to be politically correct, will not give respectful recognition to Christmas. In fact, many merchants go out of their way to disassociate their stores with Christmas. Some merchants have instructed their employees to omit a Christmas greeting in favor of a holiday greeting. Christmas trees are referred to as holiday trees and displaying a manger is politically incorrect.

It feels like these merchants, are trying to intentionally alienate Christians. If so, it is a dangerous and misguided strategy that could lead to their economic demise. I think these merchants could be playing with their financial futures, assuming the Christmas gift giving market dries up as I am going to suggest.

I encourage Christians that feel their holiday is being secularized to demonstrate their disapproval, by purchasing fewer gifts. If the majority of Christians stopped buying gifts in protest of the PC's assault on Christmas, our economy would be in shambles. It is smart to never bite the hand that feeds you. If this economic disaster should happen, you would see a tremendous change in attitude toward Christmas. I recommend that we, as Christians, be very diligent on where we spend our hard-earned, money.

Most of us in America have been blessed with an overabundance of material goods. We have more things than we know what to do with. Jesus Christ, whom the holiday is celebrating, brought a message of love and hope to humanity. Therefore, the real celebration of Christmas should reflect giving more than receiving. I believe it is our duty as Christians to help alleviate the suffering of those less fortunate and when would it be more appropriate than during Christmas?

As Christians, we should certainly not be worried about merchants making record profits but should focus our attention on helping those in need survive. Besides, there is no biblical authority for the celebration of Christmas with gift giving anyway. The pagans, who converted to Christianity, started this tradition. I believe, if we focus on gift giving and not helping humanity, we have lost the true meaning of Christmas.

Let us celebrate our savior's birth the way Jesus Christ would want us to. We should ask ourselves should it be to buy many needless gifts for each other or should we give money for the survival of those in need? Should we be giving to charities and those less fortunate in our community or try to help merchants achieve record profits?

Charities receiving hundreds of millions of dollars during the Christmas season would make much more sense than giving our money to greedy merchants. In addition to giving to the poor, Christmas is a great time to give money to our family's educational and financial needs.

Last Christmas my wife and I did not buy gifts for each other. We gave a designated amount that we would have spent on each other to a chosen charity. We both said it was the best Christmas we ever had. We have made a pledge to each other to make this an annual tradition because we are helping those in need and as a result it makes us feel so good.

Christmas is a time of joy and celebration and nothing gives more joy than giving to those who are less fortunate. I never would have thought to celebrate Christmas in this way until the controversy of Christmas started to escalate. It made me put everything into proper perspective.

My recommendation is to set aside a designated amount of money for Christmas, take a small portion and buy one gift for each family member or friend from a respectful merchant and give the remainder of the money to charity. If there is any money left over, give it in the form of savings bonds or educational funds to secure your children's future. I guarantee that when you make yearly deposits in the bank and it starts to accumulate your family will be very appreciative. I also guarantee that Christmas will come alive again. **Christmas is not about gift giving; it is about celebrating the birth of Jesus Christ our Christian savior.**

I try to put everything in a positive light. The far-left seculars have done Christians a great favor by attacking our Christmas traditions. This was not their intention but because of the controversy, all Christians can get back to the true meaning of Christmas. We must understand that we no longer live in a society where the majority rules. The politically correct seculars, with the help of liberal politicians, judges, and the ultra liberal ACLU, are quickly imposing their anti-Christian values on our society. We do not have to join them but sometimes it is easier to learn from opposing points of view.

I judge groups and organizations by their supporters more than by their detractors. Those who support the far left are usually against everything traditional. They are also very vicious in their attacks, which only confirms, my suspicions.

When the controversy first started, I have to admit that I was angry over Christmas traditions being challenged by a far-left secular minority. The more I thought about it the more I started to challenge my own traditional views. It became very clear to me that my celebration of Christmas was internal and because of this, I changed my focus. I will never again celebrate Christmas by purchasing meaningless gifts for the benefit of unappreciative merchants.

I have a business and marketing background and understand the importance of customer loyalty. Sometimes you can get better results avoiding a conflict than engaging in one. Successful merchants also understand that their businesses are enhanced when they demonstrate a sincere interest in the welfare of their customers. I for one will not try to get a merchant to respect my holiday so I can be allowed to spend my money in their store. If I feel they are being disrespectful to me for any reason, I will not shop there. As Christians, we are a huge spending block with great power.

It is very important to remember, that the politically correct seculars are anti-Christian. They are trying to secularize our Christian values. We should never compromise those values. When we give to charities, we are reinforcing our Christian faith, because faith is strengthened by good works. As Christians our primary focus should be to help those who are in need. That is a true Christmas celebration.

Christmas is a very important holiday to Christians all over the world. It is a time when all Christians should be giving their time and money to those less fortunate. If, we all joined together and started a new tradition of giving to the needy in celebration of our savior's birth, our world would be a much better place.

To gain respect we must respect ourselves. If you want all people to respect the Christmas holiday, focus on helping those in need. Those who are not Christians will also start to respect the holiday.

The merchants that want to be politically correct will be the biggest losers. Merchants not recognizing Christmas is the equivalent of cutting off your nose to spite your face. It does not make economic sense. Any merchant participating in this foolishness is playing with fire. It will serve them right, when they get burned.

CHAPTER 17

Conflict: "How To" Achieve Resolution

Conflict can be either positive or negative depending on the outcome. Effective leaders resolve conflict. Conflict is very positive when there is a goal of resolution. In this chapter, we are going to examine those groups that are successful in conflict resolution and those that are not. From the simplest to the more complicated.

The family is the least complicated yet most important group in our society. There is a head of the family who teaches discipline and demonstrates love. Morals and ethics are the foundation and are taught and encouraged in the functional family. Conflict is always confronted and resolved. Their homes are functional because the parents are effective leaders and resolve conflict. Everyone is on the same page, always communicating. President Reagan said "All great change begins at the dinner table." The functional family is the model all groups should emulate, especially Washington DC.

Successful corporations are successful because of corporate leaders that resolve conflict. These companies effectively identify areas of concern and encourage all departments to work together to ensure success. They continually look for ways to solve problems and keep their lines of communication open. Their only goal is to grow their organization and they do so by pro-actively identifying weak areas that need fixing.

They do not complain about their internal weaknesses, they repair them. Successful leadership is evaluated by their ability to continually grow their company. Strong leaders understand that the only way to succeed in business is to have company unity with a common purpose. Companies that allow conflict to escalate will eventually fail.

The functional family and successful corporations have one thing in common—they are led by strong effective leaders. These leaders encourage unity as their main source of strength. They expose problems to alleviate the problems and never try to shift the blame to someone else. They understand that they are successful only if the group they lead is successful. When they commit to these fundamentals, they epitomize success.

To understand a positive you need to sometimes expose a negative. When we discuss how important conflict resolution is for the family, team or organization to function effectively we need to also discuss how damaging unresolved conflict can be. Conflict is only positive when there is resolution otherwise it can be very damaging.

To illustrate this point there is no organization on face of this earth more inefficient and therefore less functional than our federal government. Our two parties waste all their time fighting and trying to undermine each other rather than solving problems. Abraham Lincoln said "America will never be destroyed from the outside. If we falter and lose our freedoms it will be because we destroyed ourselves."

Example: Congress passed a 2700 page Healthcare Bill for the "benefit" of the American people. They thought it was so beneficial that they exempted themselves from participating in it. I can understand why the Republicans opted out because they did not vote for the bill but if the Democrats thought it is so beneficial for America, why did they not want it for themselves?

Because most politicians are lawyers they succeeded in drawing up a 2700 page bill that is impossible to understand. In fact, House speaker Nancy Pelosi when confronted on the bill and the confusion among house members as to the verbiage of the bill said, to paraphrase, "that Congress will find out what's in it when it's passed." In other words even many in Congress did not know what they were passing to "benefit" the American people. That's our government at its worst. For Ms. Pelosi to make those comments demonstrates that she exemplifies everything that's wrong with our government.

I got a suggestion for these elitist in Washington, never pass anything for the American people that does not also pertain to them. That's called credibility!

Rather than passing a 2700 page Healthcare bill include only one sentence to describe what's in the bill: **"Everyone in Washington, with no exceptions will be obligated to participate in the same Healthcare Bill as every other American."** That would allow the "honorable" Ms. Pelosi to pass a bill without having to go behind close doors.

I would vote for that bill sight unseen if it included that one sentence. Our "ethical politicians" have never approved anything for themselves unless it was the best! Term limits anyone. Thomas Jefferson said "I predict future happiness for Americans if they can prevent the government from wasting the labors of the people under the pretense of taking care of them."

Our justice and political systems endorse and perpetuate conflict without resolution. They are so concerned about procedures, 2700 page healthcare package is an indicator, that they are blinded by their failures. They are under the false assumption that their efforts and procedures are helping our society when, in fact, they are destroying it. The problem, as I view it, is that the far left and their distorted ideology have influenced both systems negatively. Conflict without resolution is damaging.

We have discussed in this and previous chapters how the judicial system has become a procedural system. Truth is not as important as following procedures. As a result, the system has falsified its purpose.

Lawyers/politicians tell us to live by one set of principles while they live by another. For instance as lawyers they tell us how important it is for every•one to receive a fair trial and legally make the trial unfair. As I indicated many times in this book the criminal defense attorneys' goal is to prevent truthful incriminating evidence from being admissible (I'm sorry for ranting but I can't give them enough credit for their deception). The jury is then required to determine guilt or innocence, without all the evidence. That's why when they are elected to serve us in Washington they feel entitled to serve themselves.

I have come to the conclusion that the symbol of the blindfold covering the eyes of justice is an illustration of how the justice system really works. The blind fold illustrates how defense attorneys keep truthful information from the jury. I know that the judicial system would take issue with my analysis but that's what I believe our system has come to.

The judges and criminal defense attorneys have bastardized their system to their benefit. Judges have the power to interpret the laws and determine sentencing while the criminal defense attorneys have the ability to manipulate the system. Our justice system was originally designed to protect the victim and punish the guilty, but it is doing the opposite. The system has become so politically correct that it is ruining the society it was suppose to protect. Conflict is rarely resolved when truth has been compromised.

The reason I have emphasized this throughout my book is because those involved in this distorted mentality are the same ones we elect to political office. As I have stated repeatedly the vast majority of our politicians are attorneys and their sense of right and wrong defies logic. They are so use to manipulating the facts they have lost touch with reality. When lawyers are involved truth may be compromised. Our judicial and political system encourages and endorses conflict.

Lawyers are very slow to make decisions because their profession teaches them that confusion and gray are profitable. This I believe is a major reason why our immigration laws are not enforced. Their focus is on the technicalities not on the outcome. Time and confusion is money and that is why very little gets done in Washington. The Chinese general Sun Tzu said "cleverness has never been associated with long delays."

Let's look at the state of affairs facing our country. Our immigration policy is a disaster. We have at least12 million illegal immigrants from Mexico, a threat to our national security as well as a drain on our economy and our Congress does nothing. They are too busy arguing with each other to get anything done. The two political parties are bitter enemies. This has caused a very negative situation that is damaging to our country. Our enemies know that we are weak and divided and therefore vulnerable.

Both parties know the seriousness of our situation yet do little to correct it. Instead of working together to resolve these matters, they work at preventing a resolution. All they are interested in is gaining power by accusing their political rivals of ineptness as we discussed previously.

Our occupation of Iraq and Afghanistan and our immigration situation have been major contributors to this division. The far left uses these issues as excuses to vilify all those that do not agree with them. It gives them a chance to hate and that is very important to them. It is impossible to appease these far-left haters. They love to hate because it gives meaning to their meaningless lives.

The situation regarding our immigration policy cannot be clearer. As we discussed in the previous chapters we have laws regarding immigration and they cannot be more explicated. Our immigration laws are no different than Mexico or any other country. You must have documentation to enter our country. The illegal aliens do not so enforce the law. It can't be any easier yet our leaders in Washington have been unable to resolve this matter. If it is a law, enforce it if you change it change it for all.

The politically correct extremists do not want to hear opposing views because they love conflict and controversy. That is why they are considered extremists. For instance I feel many on the far left want to change and rewrite our Constitution and it scares the hell out of me.

The far left seculars of the Democratic Party have a socialist agenda and will do anything to achieve that agenda. The

Constitution of the United States is the major Core Value our country was built upon and should never be compromised. It is the major reason people from all over the world risked their lives to come to America! It is the reason our country has endured and been a shining light to the entire world. Yet the far left of the Democratic Party continually challenge many aspects of the Constitution. I predict that changing or compromising it will be our eventual downfall.

Far left extremists do not want meaningful dialog regarding the values that made our country the envy of the world. They feel our country is flawed and they are supported by far-left haters that are completely out of control with their crazy assertions.

Rosie O'Donnell, formerly a television talk show host is one of these extremists. She and others on the far left have made some of the most irresponsible statements about our military, 9/11, Iraq and Afghanistan without any credible facts to back them up. She has said that our soldiers have killed innocent victims by the hundreds of thousands.

I served in Viet Nam and our soldiers are the most humane military in the world. Because its war, at times you need to fight fire with fire and that to me is understandable but our troops rarely inflict pain on innocent victims. I don't care what the protected Rosie O'Donnell says. She has never been in an armed conflict in her life.

The war in Iraq and Afghanistan I was totally against but I am 100% for our troops. I have great compassion for each one of them because they are engaged in wars with lunatics that sacrifice their own children in the name of their distorted ideology. Our soldiers have not indiscriminately killed hundreds of thousands of civilians as Rosie claims. They have been forced to defend themselves in a hostile land where religious warfare is a way of life. She seems to have more sympathy for the enemy than for our soldiers. These religious zealots are crazy and after Saddam Hussein was over thrown mass murders and violence were eminent. She would not understand this because she is one of the protected and looks at the world through idealistic far-left glasses.

Rosie also compares Christian fundamentalists to Muslim fundamentalists, and that is like comparing the Red Cross with Dracula. Both of them take blood, only in different ways.

The Christian fundamentalists are traditional with strong moral and ethical values condemning homosexuality, abortion, etc. You may agree or disagree with them on these issues and that is certainly your right to do so but it does not give those who are in disagreement a right to misrepresent them. Christian fundamentalists do not tie explosives to their children and send them out to blow up innocent men, women, and children in the name of God.

For Rosie O'Donnell or anyone else not to see the difference in these two groups is to be in complete denial of the facts. Rosie needs to investigate Muslim Fundamentalist laws regarding the treatment of women to include honor killings, stoning, sacrificing their children and the treatment of homosexuals. After investigating if she still believes that the Christian and Muslim Fundamentalists are the same she has to be so naive and ill informed that she should not be let out of her home alone without adult supervision.

Rosie and many of her far-left supporters in Hollywood have also claimed that the US government brought down the

World Trade Center on 9/11 and not the Muslim terrorists. Rosie's hatred for former President Bush and now for President Trump has made her completely irrational and paranoid. When she is discussing these subjects, she becomes very mean spirited.

Extremists do not resolve problems, they escalate them. Extremists love conflict and controversy and never let the facts stop them from spreading their propaganda. Resolving conflict to Rosie and the far left is to continue the conflict until they prevail. There is no such thing as compromise.

The far left always complain about their lack of free speech but they are always the ones that deny free speech to anyone who opposes their viewpoint. This was never more evident than when the Minutemen visited various colleges to discuss the illegal immigration issue. Far-left students shouted them down and never gave them a chance to explain their position on immigration. The Minutemen are patriotic citizens trying to protect our borders against illegal immigrant entry. They are some of our nation's great protectors.

Many of the illegals may be gang members, drug dealers or terrorists who could destroy us. To protect our borders against attack we have to rely on the

Minutemen, who are just average citizens risking their lives to protect us because our own government , prior to Trump, was too weak and divided to do so. Yet when they go to our colleges they are shouted down. The so-called compassionate freedom of speech student activists will not let them speak. These students do not want to hear the truth if it conflicts with the ir far-left ideology. They support freedom of far-left radical speech only and are unwilling to tolerate dissent.

I bet if Fidel Castro, one of the world's great tyrants, spoke, he would be enthusiastically received. They would be so mesmerized you would be able to hear a pin drop. They would be hanging on his every word. No wonder the far left support leaders like Fidel; they emulate him and his lack of tolerance for freedom of speech.

Those in our society who talk about having compassion for the less fortunate are usually the ones with the least amount of compassion or tolerance for opposing viewpoints. Conflict can be peacefully resolved only through intelligent discussion where all points of view are calmly discussed.

I want to emphasize that Rosie O'Donnell is not alone in her criticism. Many on the far left share her sentiments and out-of-control assertions. We saw entertainers like Danny Glover hugging Hugo Chavez, and Harry Belafonte singing the praises of Fidel Castro. These entertainers talk about tolerance and aligned themselves with the most intolerant leaders. Neither of these leaders resolved conflict through discussion in their own countries. The dissidents in their countries are thrown into jail. This will become very clear when you read the chapter entitled **The Interview** at the end of my book because it was an interview with a Venezuelan citizen.

Far left activists like Danny Glover and Harry Belafonte have no credibility with me. When is the last time you saw a demonstration by the people in Cuba against their government? The Cuban people risk their lives to cross shark-infested waters to gain asylum in the United States. Again, if Cuba is such a great country, why can't the citizens of Cuba leave their country? More importantly, why do they want to leave? It is a very easy question to answer if you apply logic.

When have American citizens ever risked their lives crossing shark infested waters to gain asylum in Cuba? I am trying to figure out if these far left entertainers are stupid or trying to be manipulative by purposely distorting the truth. Are they receiving compensation for their loyalty? It is so bizarre that I can only guess as to why they embrace these tyrants.

Conflict is positive when there is a commitment to truthful communication. Conflict can be resolved only when opposing forces come together with a sincere goal of resolution. Open communication, logic and compromise are the keys to resolving conflict. That is something the far left refuse to engage in. In our nation's history, many positive outcomes have resulted when conflict was resolved through intelligent dialog.

During our country's infancy, our forefathers came together and signed the two greatest documents ever written, The Constitution and the Declaration of Independence. These documents were established and written to assure our freedoms after we gained our independence in 1776. Later in our history, President Lincoln created and signed The Emancipation Proclamation to guarantee all our citizens the freedoms that we now can take for granted. Our country was going through great turmoil during these times and yet was able to overcome these situations with positive discussion and input.

By the way these documents: The United States Constitution 6 pages, Declaration of Independence 1 page and the Emancipation Proclamation 5 pages were three of the greatest documents ever written by man and totaled 12 pages. Compare that to the 2700 page National Healthcare

Plan and you will understand why I continue to emphasize that great leader's love clarity of message. Fake leaders seek to confuse.

Presidents John F. Kennedy and Lyndon Johnson, with the help of Congress, continued to work toward total equality by enacting the 1964 Civil Rights Bill. Our country was again in great turmoil and needed to come together to ensure freedom for all. Logical people come to logical conclusions; irrational people do not.

Extremists are usually very hateful with a distorted agenda, and they limit free speech through intimidation. You can always identify them by their unwillingness to let anyone with an opposing point of view talk. They do not want to be confronted with the truth. Their ideology is so flawed that they have to try to intimidate with their passion rather than convince with their logic. They want conflict and upheaval to prevail. Their idea of resolving a conflict is when they prevent opposing points of view from being heard. The far left want you to believe they encourage freedom of speech but practice censorship.

We are a great country because of our Constitution and democracy. We encourage diversity of thought. Finding solutions to any of our problems is what made us great. When problems are not resolved, they escalate. Respectful people respect each other enough to discuss all situations with a goal of resolution. Let us not allow the ill-informed protected loud mouths to keep us from respectfully solving our problems. That is why I say we had better start shoveling the far left's ideology before it gets too deep.

Conflict with resolution is power.

CHAPTER 18

Deception

In southwest Florida there is a least one-car dealer, with various franchises, in multiple locations, that, in my opinion, does something very questionable. The dealer adds a large sum of money to the sticker price of cars and describes it as "adjusted market value." When I question the salespeople on this added expense, they try to talk around it. I have concluded that the cost added to the sticker is for having the privilege to purchase a car from them.

Deception is described as a state of being deliberately deceived. If an individual or organization has an agenda, they may resort to deception to achieve that agenda. The far left do it every day. Individuals and corporations as well as activist groups can be deceptive, especially when trying to communicate their desired goals.

My book Political Correctness is BS exposes the far left's deceptive practices and illustrates how they are negatively affecting our way of life. I have listed the twenty-five worst examples of deception in this book at the end of this chapter. Before we review the list, let's look at some other examples of the good and bad uses of deception.

In sports, we are taught at an early age, that winning requires your team to implement a strategy designed to outsmart your opposition. Like talent, strategy, plays a big part in athletic success. In baseball, the pitcher will confuse the batter by throwing a change up when he feels the batter is looking for a fastball. In football, on a third and one situation, the quarterback may fake a hand-off and throw long to fool the defense. In tennis, a drop or lob shot can be very effective in outsmarting an opponent to gain an advantage. The use of deception in sports is recognized and acceptable. It is as much a part of the game as the talented players who play it.

In business and politics, lying or cheating to gain an advantage is not an accepted practice, or at least it should not be. Those who engage in this type of deception are liars and thieves and their focus is to accomplish their goals by distorting the truth. I have illustrated throughout my book how many on the far left will do anything to achieve their agenda practice this type of deception. Most do not care how their methods and ideology affect society as long as they succeed in their efforts.

Politically correct mandated school curriculums are failing. The United States ranks twenty-fifth worldwide in education. We are at the bottom of the industrialized world in educating our children and continue to use techniques that do not work just to be politically correct.

As we discussed previously our schools teach whole language and bilingual education. It has been proven that it does not work nearly as well as using English only and phonics. Phonics helps beginners learn how to read by teaching the phonetic value of letters, which will help in the proper pronunciation of words. Yet school boards all over our country are supporting the whole language and bilingual teaching methods, which do not work, but it helps them achieve their politically correct agenda. The deception is defending this failed curriculum at the expense of our children.

When I attended school, the teachers I knew were dedicated professionals and teaching children was a labor of love. They must be horrified by the direction now taken by the school boards. School boards have sold our children out rather than be labeled politically incorrect. I always thought that schools were places of learning where dedicated teachers would do anything to help their students excel. Now schools use inadequate teaching methods that fail our children but achieve a distorted political agenda. We must not offend any minority group even if it means using inadequate teaching methods. **PC is BS**.

Profiling is another area where deception replaces logic. Profiling has become very politically incorrect by the far left protected. At our airports, those against profiling think everyone should be treated in the exact same way. The PC group believes that the eighty three year old woman who is a US citizen is just as likely a terrorist as the young Arab student. This sounds fair but is not logical. Let us look at some facts. In a Washington Post article by Emil Steiner entitled Real, Strange News, a Pew study indicates the following:

• 25% of young Muslims, under 30, in the United States believe that suicide bombing is acceptable to protect their religion (does the protecting of their religion include the killing of all non-Muslims?).

• 27% of United States Muslims refused to condemn Al-Qaeda for their terrorist attacks.

• 40% of the estimated 2.35 million American Muslims believe Arab men carried out the 9/11 bombings (how about the 60% that do not?).

I am sure if we conducted the same study with elderly

American women, their views would be much different. If these facts were known about Americans in any Arab country, do you think they would profile Americans? Any civilized country that has uncovered this type of information after 9/11 and does not profile, is just waiting for a disaster to happen. Profiling is unavoidable in our society today. Those who are against profiling are elite protected pinheads with no common sense. I am 100% in favor of profiling to protect American citizens.

Cigarette companies are another example of deception and will be among the twenty-five worst offenders listed at the end of this chapter. I cannot give them enough notoriety for their deceptive practices.

I saw an advertisement or PSA by Philip Morris telling people to go to their Web site to find out how to quit smoking. A cigarette company trying to help smokers quit. What a joke. Does anyone think that the manufacturers of cigarettes really want people to quit smoking? If everyone quit smoking, they would be out of business. They legitimize a product that addicts consumers and will eventually kill them. They have increased the amount of nicotine, which is a poisonous alkaloid found in tobacco and is very addictive, A fact that they denied in front of Congress.

Deception is who they are and represents their industry's doctrine. Nicotine is so poisonous it is used in insecticides. Yet they still manufacture this product knowing the deadly consequences. If cigarette companies really wanted to help society quit smoking, they would find a way to eliminate nicotine from their product instead of lying about its effects. If that is impossible, could they at least find ways to lessen the poisonous effects of nicotine?

Cigarettes are the only government-approved product that is guaranteed to addict you and kill you. Our government allows this product to exist because of the taxes generated by the sale of cigarettes. That is why drug dealers are outlawed in the United States: they do not share their profits with the government by way of taxes. I believe cigarettes are the most harmful product to ever receive government approval, and all the research confirms this fact.

I have always preached personal responsibility and personal responsibility is still the biggest deterrent to smoking. The problem is that when people start smoking, the cigarette companies have made it very hard for them to quit. Nicotine is an addictive drug and more deadly than most. It is like the fly that decides to fly into the spider web. Once the fly enters the web, it cannot leave. It was the fly's choice to enter the web and the spider's choice to keep it there.

If cigarette companies really wanted society to stop smoking, they would change their product. Instead, they are trying to change their image with their deceptive government-mandated stop-smoking campaigns. The campaign is meaningless, their product is deadly, and our government knows it.

We as Americans have power and the freedom of choice. We can demand that our educational system be designed to help students excel. We can demand that our borders and airports are safe by being diligent and logical. We need to demand that manufactures make products that are safe and beneficial to all consumers. We as a free democratic society should let the majority rule.

Instead, our politicians, some corporations and the far-left secular minority all with their false agendas and distorted ideology are deceiving us. Traditional values made our country strong and great. Let us not let the deceitful with their distorted propaganda and values bring us down. Remember, those who deceive have self-serving agendas and will use deception in achieving their goals. Deception is a valuable strategy in sports but a fraudulent practice in business.

I have listed twenty-five of the most deceitful practices in my book. Some we have already discussed some you will read in up-coming chapters. These are the most egregious examples of deception preformed by con artists and disguised as truth.

Before we get to review the top 25 I want to list the deception that is so egregious it must stand alone because it deceives a couple hundred million people. It is the 2700 page National Healthcare Plan passed by Congress for the "benefit" of the American people. The Democratic Congress Pass a bill that they said would "benefit" all Americans and did not know what was in it. Furthermore they exempted themselves from participating in it.

I respected Willie Sutton the famous bank robber because he used a gun to rob banks and never denied he was a criminal. Many democratic politicians were adamant on the benefits of the Plan and said it would "benefit" the people. House majority leader Nancy Pelosi knew most of them did not know its benefits because they never read it and said they will know what's in it when they pass it. Smoke and mirrors anyone? If Willie Sutton was alive and running against Nancy Pelosi I would vote for Willie. They both are con artists but one is honest enough to admit it.

Here is the top 25:

1. The judge who sued a small laundry owner for $54,000,000 because he lost his trousers

2. Rosie O'Donnell, for comparing the Christian fundamentalists with Muslim fundamentalists

3. The NAACP for defending Michael Vick

4. Danny Glover for supporting Hugo Chavez

5. The cigarette companies trying to disguise their product as legitimate

6. Corporation leaders that bankrupt their companies and cheat their employees out of millions in the name of greed

7. Michael Nifong for his intentional mishandling of the Duke Lacrosse case (upcoming)

8. Geraldo Rivera, an activist, for posing as an unbiased journalist

9. The art director who defended the artwork displaying the Holy Bible being flushed down the toilet as free speech

10. The Muslims in England who organized a "religion of peace rally" that called for the beheading of non-Muslims

11. Former Syracuse University Chancellor Buzz Shaw for canceling the Boy Scouts' annual fund-raising dinner because the Scouts do not accept homosexual leaders (upcoming)

12. The ACLU for supporting every far-left group that attacks Judeo-Christian values

13. The Mexican-American leadership that organizes illegal immigrants to oppose our nation's laws

14. The criminal defense attorneys who represented Muslim

clerics who were suing US Airways and their passengers for profiling

15. The far left who demand freedom of speech and shouted down the Minutemen who tried to discuss immigration

16. Politicians in both parties who defend their parties' indiscretions while attacking their rivals for their indiscretions

17. The leaders who change their standards of justice when they or their group is accused of a crime

18. Criminal defense attorneys who justify their manipulation of our court system

19. Major league baseball for its handling of the illegal drug issue (upcoming)

20. To all those who defended a Democratic representative who was found with $90,000 in his freezer (upcoming)

21. Multi-million dollar athletes who accuse their teams of racism

22. The far left in Hollywood who supported and endorsed Fidel Castro

23. President Carter for criticizing any president's job performance (upcoming)

24. Far-left mandated school curriculums

25. The groups that expect preferential treatment because of their politics, color, or sexual preference

I had a hard time listing just twenty-five of these deceptive practices; there could have been many more. The majority of my list, as well as my book, are composed of far-left activist ideology. They have a flawed ideology that they try to impose on the rest of us. It is anti-traditional and devoid of truth and common sense.

We must demand that the truth always take precedence over distorted ideology.

CHAPTER 19

Abortion/Abortionolics

Abortion is very controversial and that's why I included it in my book. Each side of the abortion issue is very passionate in its beliefs. On one side, those who support abortion feel it's a woman's right to do what she wants with her body. On the other side, they feel that abortion is murder. Both sides are, as I said, very passionate on this issue. Unfortunately, neither side will listen to the others point of view.

In chapter 16 I discussed the importance of conflict resolution. When a conflict is unable to be resolved it escalates and becomes more controversial. Information stimulates thought and thought stimulate ideas especially when it is accurate information. I will propose a solution later in this chapter on "how to" obtain accurate information to resolve this conflict.

Many pro-abortionists object to any limitations on abortion. They feel that even late-term abortions are permissible. They believe very strongly that it is a women's body and therefore her right to choose. Pro-abortionists feel that abortion is a freedom issue and not a right to life issue. I think the problem is that it's both.

Many anti-abortionists feel it is a religious issue. They refer to biblical passages to support their point of view. They feel that the fetus in the womb is a child and should be protected. In fact, many anti-abortionists refer to Jeremiah 1:5 (Old Testament) to support their beliefs. It says, "Before I formed you in the womb I knew you, and before you were born I consecrated you." This statement is very powerful especially for those who believe that the Bible is the living word of God.

Anti-abortionists, feel so strongly about this issue that they have picketed abortion clinics trying to intimidate doctors as well as patients. A couple of very radical antiabortionists have even murdered doctors who perform abortions and clinic personnel. Thankfully, they are the rare exceptions but that is how crazy this controversy has become.

The legalization of abortion is very controversial in itself. In 1973, the Supreme Court legalized abortion with Roe vs. Wade. The court's decision was based on a vague right of privacy not spelled out in the Constitution. The Supreme Court was legislating social policy and exceeding its authority as interpreter of the law. The central issue at hand is whether the live child in the womb has Constitutional rights. The Supreme Court decided they did not.

Most of us who have tried to formulate an opinion on this issue without understanding all the facts have become confused. Confusion can lead to apathy, which is an effective strategy used by lawyers and activist groups to help them achieve their agendas. If society is not aware of the long-term negative consequences resulting from the decisions they make, they can be easily manipulated. It is very easy to distort the facts when you limit information.

There is an old saying that a little knowledge is a dangerous thing and that is absolutely true, especially in the case of abortion. Our judicial procedural system with its loophole-savvy attorneys is a testament to how effective a strategy of limiting information can be. Information is the most important element needed to be able to arrive at logical conclusions.

I feel that pro-abortion activist groups have purposely tried to limit information regarding abortions. Abortion activists do not tell the whole story; they focus only on the right of the women to choose. They do not focus on the procedure or the condition of the fetus before, during, or after the procedure. Limiting information has always been a key element in the far left activist's strategy.

For this reason, we should provide society with as much information as possible on this issue and to do so, my recommendation would be to show abortions on television. If the fetus comes out as a mass of tissue, the pro-abortionist will win over the majority of public opinion. Most will agree that it is a woman's body, and it is her choice. If the fetus comes out developed, with arms, legs, fingers, and even fingernails, etc., then the anti-abortionist will gain public support.

Some people may say that showing an abortion on television is barbaric. If any medical procedure is too barbaric to show on television then it just may be too barbaric to perform. Besides, they now show all kinds of medical procedures on television daily. Everything from heart transplants to amputations. The public is becoming immune to the sight of medical procedures.

I have never seen an abortion and do not know all the facts. I don't know what happens if the baby happens to come out alive. I don't know what they do with the discarded fetus or what it looks like after the procedure and, therefore, I am not emotionally involved in the controversy. Showing it on television with a doctor explaining the entire procedure will at least give society enough information to formulate an intelligent opinion.

I will guarantee you that the vast majority of pro-abortionists have never witnessed an abortion. Truthful non-censored information is a wonderful thing. It allows people to arrive at educated decisions that they can feel comfortable with.

My recommendation seems simple enough so why do you think that abortions are not shown on television? Could it be that some political groups don't want the public to have all the facts regarding abortion? If millions witnessed the entire abortion procedure, including the discarding of the fetus, would that influence and change societies mind on this issue? Would those contemplating the procedure think differently about their decision? We all have to live by the decisions we make long after we make them. Important life-changing decisions require factual information.

Are we allowing the far-left politically correct activists again, to intimidate our thought process? Women's rights groups are very powerful and are pro-choice and that is their prerogative. They should strongly defend the positions that they believe in. That does not give them the right to distort or prevent the abortion issue from being thoroughly examined. I am always suspicious when the far-left politically correct get involved, especially when they are supported by the judicial system.

Distorted political agendas presented by loud aggressive political activists groups seem to have great influence on our politicians/lawyers. It frightens them to death. I have tried to illustrate throughout my book how the far left demand free and open speech yet try to censor any speech and attack those that opposes their ideology.

Remember, keeping the truth from the jury is how criminal defense attorneys make their living. Keeping the truth from society will lead to our demise. We continue to let the judicial process/mentality and the far-left politically correct influence us. Many in our society let aggressive behavior by those without values compromise their beliefs. If you do not stand for something, you stand for nothing.

When you give society all the information needed, people will come up with well-thought-out scenarios. For me to feel comfortable about the decisions I make, I need information. There will be fewer issues such as abortion if all the facts are readily available to the public. Abortion is a very serious matter and should be examined thoroughly. Controversial subjects remain controversial because of a lack of information.

In my book, chapter after chapter, I refer to how the far left and the judicial system have had a negative influence on our society by focusing on proper procedures rather than truth. When the truth is omitted, issues are rarely resolved and, in fact, preventing all the information from being considered will actually help to expand the controversy.

When researching this subject I found that one key word is usually missing when people discuss abortion and that word is "responsibility." The fact is that there have been nearly fifty million abortions performed in the United States since it was legalized in 1973. That number is staggering. Intelligent men and women have to take responsibility for their actions. If they engage in unprotected sex, they should understand the consequences. Not only are they risking their lives, there is a good chance of a pregnancy. Having multiple abortions because you cannot control yourself is not only irresponsible, it may be life threatening. Sexually transmitted diseases can be very dangerous.

I know that many women feel it is their body to do what they want with but along with a body goes a brain. Fifty million abortions is a national disgrace, and I am not even dogmatic on the abortion issue, or I should say, I was not until I researched these figures.

Anyone that endorses and encourages unlimited abortions I refer to as abortionolics. Their far left ideology has replaced common sense. I am sure that the vast majority of abortionolics have never witnessed an actual abortion and have no idea what they are advocating. Until they do I suggest they proceed with caution.

If we applied the same logic to the legalization of the death penalty and in thirty plus years fifty million convicts were executed there would be a national outcry and rightly so. It would not matter if these convicts were all rapists and murders accused of committing horrific crimes, there would still be national condemnation, especially from our friends on the far left. Society would feel that fifty million executions were excessive yet most in society remain silent on the abortion issue.

We may have aborted some babies that if they lived may have achieved greatness as scientists or as humanitarians. For me 50 million abortions is more than a protest its wholesale murder. If all those in favor of abortions actually saw the innocent remains of the babies slaughtered they may come to understand the consequences of their ideology. It is a modern day holocaust and for those of us that have faith to remain silent and without objection is, I believe, compromising our faith. TV exposure may help bring clarity to this devastation.

We have no idea who has been destroyed as a result, of our wholesale abortion policy.

There are too many responsible ways to prevent a pregnancy, to allow this number of abortions to continue. Many of those who endorse wholesale abortions are far-left seculars with a distorted agenda.

They are devoid of a moral or religious conscience and believe convenience has priority over the consequences of their actions.

CHAPTER 20

Hypocrisy

As you continue to read my book you are witnessing first hand the great concerns I have with our judicial and political systems. I cannot give them enough recognition for our countries continual demise. To stay honest to myself I have to include them in every chapter because both systems are involved in everything that happens in America and that is a big part of the problem.

The ridiculous has become the norm and the normal has become non-traditional. If a parent spanks their child they can be brought up on charges. A thirteen year old female child can have an abortion without their parent's permission. A criminal can sue their victims if they are hurt during their crime spree as we witnessed in chapter 3. Wrong has become right and right has become wrong and it's all due to our upside down judicial/political systems.

I feel this has happened because truth has been compromised in place of procedures. Whenever truth is omitted from any equation the outcome is fraudulent. In this chapter I will again give examples of the lawyers/politicians sense of fairness. The politically correct activists groups whom I also challenge benefit from this hypocrisy but are the result not necessarily the cause.

Did you ever notice that it is usually the most disrespectful people who complain about being disrespected? If you want to be treated with respect, be respectful. Truth is always based on fair and equal treatment of everyone. Creating a double standard to try to remedy past wrongs is unfair. Credibility is based on your actions, not on your observations.

In 2006 Democrats were complaining about the corruption of some of their Republican counterparts and rightly so. Some Republicans were in compromising positions with lobbyists, pages, etc. These Republicans breached the voters' trust and the Democrats were outraged. It was nasty and the Republicans who were in violation were voted out of office.

So when the Democrats took over, what did they do? For one thing, they appointed a Democratic representative chair of a committee even though he had been found with $90,000 hidden in his freezer. It destroyed their credibility. I was hoping for so much more.

Hypocrisy is committed in Washington by both parties and all they do is point fingers. When President Obama was a candidate he took issue with ear marks accompanying most bills and said it would never happen in his administration. So after he was elected one of the first bills he signed had over three thousand ear marks included.

Congress voted to deny a cost of living increase for social security recipients for a two year period because of our country's financial situation while voting themselves a raise. I am very confused I thought they worked for us. A Washington insider once told me that Capitol Hill is known as "The Last Plantation" to the insiders. Now I know why!

My definition of politics is hypocrisy and it happens every day. Both parties look under a magnifying glass at their rival's character, while defending and justifying their party's outlandish behavior. We previously discussed how the Democratic majority in Congress passed a 2700 page healthcare bill that they hailed as "beneficial" for Americans and voted not to participate in it themselves. In fact most had never even read this "beneficial" bill.

Hypocrisy can also happen when you attack someone's character. You run the risk of sounding mean spirited. I am a leadership, sales and marketing consultant so prior to the 2004 presidential election, I contacted the chairman of the Democratic Party in my hometown to offer my consulting services for the upcoming presidential election. I felt 2004 was a slam dunk for the Democrats. They could not lose.

Prior to the 2004 presidential election President Bush had six months that you would not want to wish on anyone. I thought the whole country was eager for a change so I wrote a letter to the head of the DNC, Terry McAuliffe. He never responded. I think he was overconfident and did not feel he needed help.

Their eventual strategy was to personally attack the character and ethics of then President Bush. It was what the far-left element of their party wanted. The more viscous the personal attack the better they liked it. It made them feel good. It energized the far left and cost the Democrats the election.

It was a mindless strategy. They wanted the nation to know how much they despised the President and, in turn, actually helped elect him. Satan was not as bad as their portrayal of George W. Bush. When you get so emotional about anyone, it starts to affect your common sense. When this happens, you can start to become paranoid. Paranoia gives way to hysteria and leads to irrational behavior and poor judgment.

When you occasionally speak well of your opponent's character and take issue with his or her political strategies you will get most people's attention. Most unbiased, educated people know that both parties, Republicans and Democrats, will do anything to gain power. Their tactics mirror each other. They will accuse their rivals of misconduct and exonerate themselves when confronted with the same misconduct.

What voters are looking for is someone who has strong conviction and a kind spirit ready to unite not divide. When you are always attacking someone's character you better make sure your slate is clean. Besides, personal attacks will help your opponent by re-energizing their base and that's the last thing you want to do in politics. In my opinion, that is exactly what happened in the 2004 election.

Strength and kindness are very appealing and a simple but great strategy.

I do not necessarily think Senator John Kerry would have made a bad president. He just made a bad candidate. He was always angry and continually attacked George W. Bush by name. Former President Bush, on the other hand, always referred to him as my opponent. It is a kinder way of getting your point across.

The Democrats' hatred for George W. Bush cost them the election. When potential voters always hear the opposing party criticize a candidate's character, never saying a kind word, it is a turnoff. Most people are aware of how each party positions itself favorably and its rivals unfavorably. The hypocrisy becomes apparent when they will always accuse their rivals and never take responsibility for their questionable actions.

Let the discussion focus on the issues, not on how much you despise your opponent. In fact, occasionally say something nice about your opponent and most people will find you appealing.

In politics, we see how hypocrisy is a way of life. There is no greater example of that than former President Jimmy Carter and his attacks on former President Bush. In my opinion, President Charter was probably the worst president in the last one hundred years. He could not make a decision, mortgage interest rates were the highest in history and we were considered so weak around the world that Iran took over our embassy. Yet he criticized President Bush every day. Every time he would mention former President Bush, it reminded me how awful his presidency was. If he would just keep his mouth shut, maybe we would forget.

Former President Gerald Ford was certainly not a great president. The difference is he did not feel qualified to attack other presidents on their performance because of his lack of performance and, therefore, was not hypocritical. I know he was not effective as a president but I forgot in what areas.

How about the late Senator Ted Kennedy, who use to always refer to the Republican Party as the big business party catering to the rich. How many Republicans have the Kennedy wealth? Ted Kennedy was a rich, rich man. The family owns oil wells and is certainly into big business. The late Senator did a lot for the people of Massachusetts and I'm not trying to minimize his legacy but his constant attacks on "the wealthy" were disingenuous.

Politicians in both parties always engage in hypocrisy. That is a big part of what they do well and that is also why I have to include them and their tactics in every chapter.

The all-time example of hypocrisy though is Hollywood. The Hollywood insiders called former President Bush and his administration names such as stupid, morons, and idiots. Whenever you call someone a name you should make sure your background reflects strength in that area—if not, it is hypocrisy. Case in point, if you call someone stupid you'd better have a good education.

Let's look at the protected Hollywood accusers and those politicians they accuse and compare their "formal education." The three most notable politicians in the Republican Party who, during the Bush administration were most responsible for most decisions made by the administration were former President George W. Bush, Vice President Dick Cheney, and National Security Advisor Condoleezza Rice. All three were part of an administration that was always being criticized for its handling of our nation's problems.

Many on the far left in Hollywood questioned the logic used by this administration in most foreign and domestic decisions they rendered. Many entertainers feel that they are more qualified to make these decisions. They must feel their superior intelligence and political experience enable them to better understand the problems of our world.

Let us look at both groups and determine which group is more qualified to make these political decisions based solely on their political experience and educational background.

We will start with former President Bush: Graduated Yale University MBA, Harvard Business School

Elected to two terms as governor of Texas— second term received 49% Hispanic, 27% African American, 27%

Democratic and 65% of the women's vote. He also served as a pilot, flying the F102s in the Texas National guard. Former Vice President Dick Cheney:

Studied at Yale University, Casper University, and University of Wyoming where he graduated with a BA in 1965 and an MA in 1966. Studied political science at the University of Wisconsin and won American Political Science Award Former National Security Advisor Condoleezza Rice: BA Political Science Cum Laude and Phi Beta Kappa, University of Denver 1974

I have now randomly picked nine Hollywood actors who have been very insulting to the former president for his lack of intelligence and want to compare their education and political backgrounds. Remember these accusers are always using the word stupid when referring to the president. Here we go:

Barbara Streisand—High School graduate

Cher—Dropped out of High School at 16years old

Jessica Lange—Dropped out of college first year

Julia Roberts—High school graduate

Ed Asner—High school graduate

Michael Moore—Dropped out of Michigan University first year

Sarah Jessica Parker—High school graduate

Alec Baldwin—College dropout, after a scandal

George Clooney—Dropped out of college

Not exactly a who's who of academic achievement. In addition, none of these Hollywood know-it-alls has ever been elected to any political office.

Most celebrities tell us how to live, and if we do not conform to their far left PC protected view of the world, we are looked down upon. They criticize our government and our society and yet are socially and morally dysfunctional. They are the epitome of hypocrisy. Being a far-left activist does not mean you are an expert. It only means that you think you are.

Hollywood will probably argue that George W. Bush, the student, was given special treatment to help him graduate. Yale is a very prestigious university and is, in my opinion, beyond reproach. It would be more likely that a lesser college would compromise its values, not Yale.

When actress Jessica Lange was in Spain in September of 2002 she called President Bush many names and said that she was embarrassed to be an American because of this president being in office. My answer to that is that I am embarrassed that she is an American making these statements.

Someone once said when you point your finger at someone you have three pointing back at you. Ronald Reagan left the White House with a 62% favorable rating. It was said that he never made an adversary an enemy. It is a good rule to follow.

Sun Tzu said, "Never surround an army because a desperate foe is too dangerous a foe." I feel the same way about people. Do not attack people's character without giving them some slack. It leaves them only one way out through you.

Another good rule to follow is to be candid about your own shortcomings before criticizing others. It makes you very credible. When you occasionally say something negative about your performance, it gives you credibility. When you are always pointing at others and never at yourself, you lose credibility.

Another great example of hypocrisy is Ted Haggard the evangelist minister who preached against homosexuality as a sin while having a homosexual affair. I guess to him, it was only a sin for everyone else.

Be very careful before pointing your finger in condemnation; remember, when you do you will have three fingers pointing back at you. Get your own house in order before accusing others. Be kind in your approach and strong in your character and most people will find you very credible and appealing. If you want to ensure your credibility, study the actions of the far-left activist or our politicians and do the exact opposite.

CHAPTER 21

Ethics, Morals and Integrity

The dictionary states that integrity means incorruptibility. The synonym of integrity is honesty. People with strong moral and ethical principles and uncompromising values have integrity. Morals, ethics, and integrity are one in the same. You cannot claim one without the others. People and organizations with integrity are committed to telling the truth in spite of the circumstances they face. Integrity means keeping your word and doing what is right. Do you have the courage of your convictions?

Unfortunately, in our superficial society, we witness many people and institutions who claim to have integrity, compromise their standards whenever they feel it is necessary to do so. In our far-left politically correct world, influenced by the criminal justice system, integrity means not being convicted of your crime. Judicial justice has little to do with ethics, morals, and integrity.

When you cheat to accomplish your goals, and succeed in doing so, it encourages more cheating. Once this happens, it becomes a way of life. It takes someone with great character to stay morally strong in our superficial, permissive society because style is preferred over substance. Every day we hear factual accounts of corporate executives, politicians, activist groups, the judicial system, and even baseball, our national pastime, in compromising positions.

Executives at corporations such as Enron, WorldCom,

and Adelphia have all been caught cheating employees and stockholders. They have engaged in creating inaccurate accounting information designed to inflate their companies' worth. Employee pension funds have been lost because of these fraudulent business practices, leaving their dedicated employees with nothing. Dishonest people in the name of greed perpetrated this deception. They are no different from the politicians who shout their virtues then lie about their business and personal affairs. This has become commonplace in our PC society.

We witnessed this some years ago with former President Bill Clinton when he lied about having an affair with an intern. When he was confronted with the truth, he and his supporters cried foul. They said that he did not have to disclose his affair because it was a personnel thing and had nothing to do with politics. In other words, it is acceptable for the president of the United States to engage in oral sex in the White House with an intern and then lie about it. I wonder if it would have been all right if the opposing party was caught in the same compromising position?

It is another example of how politicians justify their unethical, immoral behavior when it is convenient for them to do so. No wonder so many in our society find it so easy to avoid responsibility by denying the truth. They have great role models to emulate.

The far-left activist groups also engage in unethical behavior, only they do it by using half-truths and intimidation to impose their agendas. They often take research out of context to fit into their far-left ideology. Consider their admiration for leaders like Fidel Castro and Hugo Chavez who are viewed as heroes by the far left and tyrants to their own people. The far left support these tyrants because they will investigate an issue only long enough to justify their ideology. They discourage diversity of thought if it does not agree with their ideology and use verbal intimidation to achieve their goals, and that is fraudulent.

Our judicial system's loss of integrity has had the most damaging effect on society. It has become a procedural system and has little to do with right and wrong. Criminal defense attorneys use every procedure in the book to prevent truthful, incriminating evidence from ever entering the courtroom. They have created a system void of integrity.

Our judicial system was originally designed to keep society safe; instead it is being manipulated and rewarding the criminals and their attorneys. In my opinion, the criminal defense attorneys have become the criminals. I know I have driven this theme home throughout my book but I cannot stress enough the negative impact our failed justice system has had on our society.

The O.J. Simpson case was an example of a complete sham disguised as a fair trial. His defense attorneys used procedural manipulation to get a not guilty verdict. The jury was rigged with biased jurors who favored Mr. Simpson and the defense prior to the trial. They never would have convicted O.J Simpson solely on the bases of his color.

The jury consultants who were hired by these defense attorneys determined the outcome of the trial when they chose these jurors. In my opinion, his attorneys committed white-collar fraud and corruption. It was a travesty disguised as truth and is commonplace in the courtroom.

Those defense attorneys who engage in these practices

are very arrogant and without souls. If their families were the victims and had to endure this type of injustice, they would be the first ones to shout their disapproval. They have become so distorted that they defend their ethics, morals and integrity when engaging in these deceitful practices. In other words they have become delusional, unable to distinguish right from wrong.

Even our national pastime baseball has compromised its integrity by its failure to enforce its own rules. The baseball union, run by lawyers, has ensured this compromise. A clear example of this happened some years ago during a playoff series when a player objected to an umpire's call and spit in the umpires face. The player was allowed to continue to play the entire playoff series. His penalty was to be suspended the first six games of the following season. How ridiculous to be suspended at the start of the next season; it amounts to not being suspended at all. The players' union backed the player and demanded he play the remaining playoff games. The wimpy baseball owners agreed to this foolishness. The owners' lack of integrity in the face of opposition has created a monster.

For me now as a former fan, baseball records mean little to nothing. Baseball policies lack enforcement and without enforcement they are meaningless.

Let us look at how it has affected sports' most coveted achievement, the single season and career home-run records. The pursuit of these records used to be the most coveted and acclaimed accomplishment in all of sports. Now it is the subject of jokes and it is easy to understand why.

Major League Baseball has a policy against players using

performance-enhancing drugs. Yet, Roger Maris' single season home run record was broken by suspected drug-enhanced users. Mark McGwire hit seventy home runs in a single season to first break the single season record, but he was refused entry into the Baseball Hall of Fame because of strong evidence indicating he used performance-enhancing drugs. McGwire is the only player with 580 lifetime home runs or more to be denied by the Hall of Fame committee, and the vote was not even close.

The commissioner of baseball and those associated with enforcing the rules turned their backs and refused to address the issue so the Hall of Fame committee did. I am glad someone associated with baseball showed some integrity.

To make matters worse for baseball, Barry Bonds, another strongly suspected steroid abuser broke Hank Aaron's all-time home run record and Mc Gwire single season record. When Bonds broke the records baseball celebrated.

What a joke. Prior to 2001, Bonds had never had a fifty plus home run season. In fact, let us look at the numbers. From his rookie year in 1986 to 1999, Barry Bonds hit 455 home runs in his first fourteen seasons in the major leagues. That is an average of 32.5 home runs per year. From 2000–2004 he hit 258 home runs at an average of 51.6 home runs per seasons, including his record-breaking 2001 season of seventy-three home runs. In 2007 Bonds became the new "homerun" king. What a surprise and baseball will tell you that it had nothing to do with steroids.

Most normal athletes decline in production the older they get—but not Bonds. I wonder why he was getting stronger with age while the rest of society gets weaker with age.

In my opinion, baseball, to create excitement over the home run records, has completely lost its ethics, morals and integrity. I know professional sports are a big business but it is also a spectator sport and fans need to respect it. I for one have lost all respect for baseball. I also predict that Bonds' lawyers will make it very difficult for him to ever be indicted for this abuse. We may never know the real story. Which in and of itself is the story. Isn't our judicial system grand?

Fortunately, not all sports are as blatantly unethical as baseball has become through weak enforcement and leadership. Baseball Commissioner Bud Selig did not step up and face the controversy. If this controversy is ever resolved, it will not be due to the efforts of people like Bud Selig. It will be in spite of them.

Sports, as well as industry, are subjected to judicial scrutiny. I said earlier that lawyers are involved in every business. They write the procedures on how to operate a business according to judicial specifications. They are the only entity that monitors every business in America as to their ethical practices.

The problem is that everything has become complicated. If you sell your house you have to hire a lawyer to help in finalizing the sale. They will create a huge document to ensure the sale. I have always felt that if I had the title to my house and the buyer had the money and we exchanged the two it would result in a sale. That type of archaic reasoning is discouraged in our overly complicated judicial environment.

Why do you think it is so complicated to sell your home? Is it because confusion and complexity create income for lawyers? I am always suspicious when anything is too detailed. When I am required to read the fine print I feel I better hold on to my wallet.

In America lawyers monitor all businesses to determine the credibility of their business and industry practices. The problem is that they also monitor themselves. They are the only industry that makes their own rules and monitors them. Lawyers have a strong lobby in Washington and most politicians are lawyers. They make the rules for everyone including themselves.

Power corrupts especially when those in power can judge their ethics, morals and integrity. This happened when Congress passed the Healthcare bill. The democrats were two votes short of passage so they bribe two senators to change their "no" votes to "yes." Nebraska senator Ben Nelson and Louisiana senator Mary Landrieu both were given political bribes to change their votes. When their party was questioned on these tactics they said "that's how business is done in Washington."

If any business in American other than Congress engaged in these fraudulent practices they would be put in jail. Those that endorse and participate in this deceit are criminals that have legalized their own crimes. They have sold their integrity and lost their morals and ethics. Only lawyers can justify this type of con. Remember they are the only ones in America that create, develop and monitor themselves. Do you think there will ever be court reform?

Keeping your integrity is what moral and ethical people do in spite of their situation and the pressure that is being applied. When our most sacred institutions are compromised, it has a negative affect on our entire society. People start to wonder if they are fools to play by the rules.

In the distant past, I use to revere our great institutions like our colleges, judicial and political systems, and even our national pastime, baseball. I used to think these institutions were beyond reproach and truth would never be compromised. Instead, we see the opposite, where they compromise integrity for political correctness. We are becoming unethical robots afraid to stand for the truth.

To defend ethics, morals and integrity is an honor; to compromise them is a disgrace.

CHAPTER 22

Arrogance

In our politically correct society arrogance is away of life, especially with the far left. The dictionary says the meaning of arrogance is to dispose or exaggerate one's own worth or importance in an overbearing manner. Arrogant people are boastful and very difficult to associate with. The epitome of arrogance though is when you purposely distort the truth, then vehemently defend your distortions. When you think, you are never wrong in your assumptions and therefore refuse to let anyone speak who disagrees. The judicial system and the far-left activist groups are guilty of both.

I felt compelled in my book to highlight individuals and groups that I believe are interested only in themselves. They do not care about how their actions affect those around them. They are too busy focusing on their own interests and desires. They are so self absorbed that they will justify their actions no matter how bizarre the outcome.

I am also going to give an example of individuals who are humble in their demeanor so we can draw a clear comparison. Each characteristic exposes the other because sometimes it is difficult to recognize bad behavior until you witness the good.

Sports, Hollywood, and the out-of-control judicial system are going to be my primary areas of attention. Athletes and actors have a great impact on today's youth because their adoring public gives them so much notoriety. When they step out of their areas of expertise and try to become experts on politics or life, they demonstrate a great arrogance. They are exaggerating their own worth and importance.

In the sports world we see humble athletes perform with talent and grace. These are a rare breed of athletes nowadays who are outstanding in their field of endeavor yet gracious when receiving acknowledgement for their performance. To me, in our superficial society, that type of individual is very special. Players like Marvin Harrison of the Indianapolis Colts, Michael Jordan, Phil Mickelson, Wayne Gretzky, and Tim Duncan were all great athletes who always demonstrate dignity and class. They are all standouts in their field yet humble in their demeanor. They do not ridicule their opponents. Watching them perform is a beautiful thing.

Let's compare them to many famous athletes or entertainers from yesterday and today who are in love with themselves. Muhammad Ali was a great boxer who was the epitome of arrogance. He was so boastful that he tried to humiliate every opponent he ever fought, while always glorifying himself. He even coined the phrase "I am the greatest," which takes arrogance to an all-time low level. Unfortunately, his behavior has created a legion of arrogant athletes who have followed his lead. I know some people find this amusing and nowadays they expect this type of behavior from most athletes. I think it is very distasteful and classless.

When you find it necessary to belittle your opponent before and after a victory while always glorifying yourself, the problem lies within you. It usually demonstrates a tremendous need for attention. Maybe that is why many athletes refer to their sporting event as "show time." They are just dying for the attention. Ali made this type of behavior credible. I thought Ali was a truly great fighter—but a terrible role model.

He certainly exaggerated his own worth or importance in an overbearing manner. After all he was just a professional boxer he was not going help mankind by curing cancer.

When you are blessed with talent from God, be very thankful for it. Do not humiliate others with less talent. Part of having class is being thankful for your situation, not putting down others who are less fortunate. Having to brag about yourself lessens your accomplishments in the eyes of others. Having those who observe your achievement give recognition for your success is virtuous praise.

In college basketball, there have been many great coaches. Those who not only know the X's and O's but also have the ability to develop talented players into a cohesive winning team. Three coaches who stand out to me for their ability to win consistently are the late John Wooden, Dean Smith, and Bobby Knight. All three coaches have been very successful in developing winning programs.

Coaches Wooden and Smith were disciplined men with strong values and great character. They not only helped create winning teams but also helped develop their players into good citizens. Great leaders are judged on their ability to improve the skills and behavior of those they lead. Both coaches helped their players become better citizens. They demonstrated dignity and respect for their players, fans, and opponents. Both were a true credit to coaching.

Bobby Knight is also a successful coach who has a different reflection. His arrogance is so unbecoming it takes away from his achievements. On the plus side, his student athletes have a very high graduation rate and this can be directly attributed to his emphasis on education. Most college basketball players do not go into the pros, so graduating is very important and Coach Knight stressed education.

On the other side of the ledger, he always has to play the tough guy role. He always has a scowl on his face and looks like he is mad at the world. He is rude and confrontational with everyone who tries to interview him. He called sportswriters names and tries to make those who ask tough questions look stupid. I have seen him walk out of interviews if he does not like the questions people ask. Bobby Knight is very much impressed with Bobby Knight.

With all his success on the court and his players' high graduation rate, I still think he is bad for college basketball. He is certainly not a positive role model. I do not know why it took Indiana University so long to fire him. Webster's definition of arrogance certainly defines Bobby Knight.

The leaders that I admire most are those that lead by example, develop talent, motivate through recognition, discipline non-performance and are strategic planners always focused on team unity. When the focus is on helping others succeed by developing their talent and improving their behavior your role as a leader is solidified. Coach Smith and Wooden spent their career improving the lives of those that interacted with them. They are the antithesis of arrogance and their legacies will live forever in college basketball.

Arrogance happens when someone is so self absorbed they inflate their own worth. I had someone once give me some great advice he said "you know when you know you're in big trouble? When you start believing all the nice things people say about you." Its great advice that I did not always take seriously but I should have.

We have had entertainers who have shown great arrogance. A couple of famous entertainers even threatened to move out of the United States if George W. Bush was reelected president. Are they kidding? Do they think anyone really cares where they live? To make that statement you have to be so self-absorbed that it is beyond most people's comprehension including theirs. In addition these entertainers, mostly on the far left; think they know more about politics than the electorate.

Many in Hollywood are rich yet they embrace farleft socialist leaders who have created third-world economies for those desperate folks they lead. Hollywood's far-left ideology does not make sense. They live lavishly and endorse socialistic leaders who reject capitalism. They are phony, because they do not live the lives they endorse. They hate our capitalistic society while richly benefiting from it. In other words their far left philosophy is good to preach and uncomfortable to live. Their arrogance is in exaggerating their importance and knowledge.

Now I am going to discuss who I believe are the most arrogant people of all, the high-priced criminal defense attorneys. They knowingly defend criminals who have cheated or violated innocent victims and use every "legal procedure" possible to allow their clients to escape justice. The criminal defense attorney makes a mockery of the criminal justice system by distorting the truth. Then, in their arrogance, they vehemently defend their distortions and condemn everyone else for questioning their tactics. Even when they know their clients were guilty and escaped justice through a technicality. They defend injustice and are belligerent when doing so.

If this same form of injustice were inflicted on their family, they would be outraged. If the definition of arrogance is to exaggerate one's own worth or importance in an overbearing manner, who would be more deserving to be labeled as "arrogant" than criminal defense attorneys? They are the epitome of arrogance.

My book is about how the far-left politically correct are ruining America. I included this chapter because arrogance and the far left are closely associated. In fact, I think they are one in the same.

Arrogant people feel that their views and opinions mean more than anyone else's. They will do anything to achieve their distorted agendas. Arrogance is thinking you have all the answers.

The radical far left are convinced that they are always right on every subject. Hollywood and the judicial system are a big part of the far-left arrogance.

Dignified classy people are humble with strong character. They do not brag about themselves and are very appreciative for what they have been able to accomplish. They are always ready to give recognition to others for their achievements. When competing, they try hard to win but never try to humiliate.

When people have great talent and great humility, they are very charismatic. People want them to win, and will rally behind them to ensure success. Humility is a blessing and arrogance is a curse. Humble people rarely tell everyone else how to live. Only arrogant people do. Humble people can admit their mistakes; arrogant people cannot. Humble people discuss and encourage different opinions; arrogant people shout down their detractors. Humble people are modest; arrogant people are braggarts.

When I do my seminars, I define class and character differently from our superficial society. Many in our society have come to define class by the type of car someone drives or by the clothes they wear. My definition is that classy people treat all people with dignity and respect. Having class is defined by how you treat others, not by what you own. Humility and class are synonymous. Things are superficial nonsense and any idiot can own things.

We are all blessed with talent so keep everything in perspective and do not fall in love with yourself. Encourage input and keep an open mind before you make a decision. Research a subject before you become an authority. Demonstrate courtesy by allowing and encouraging others to voice their opinions. You may actually learn something. Remember, humility is a blessing, arrogance is a curse.

CHAPTER 23

Perception (Believe it or not)

The main topic in my book is how the politically correct far left's distortion of the truth is ruining America. It is helping these anti-traditionalists with a false agenda succeed in changing our perceptions. To be politically correct is to compromise our ethics, morals and integrity. The far left are trying to force their ideals on the rest of us through intimidation by changing our perception of good and evil.

Perception happens when you form a mental image of something. The mental image can be based on research, speculation, or just plain bias. False information will lead to a false conclusion. Creating your perception is much easier to formulate if you want something to be true. For example, when the far left say that the Bush administration was responsible for murdering six hundred thousand innocent Iraq civilians and you hate the administration, you may believe the accusation because you want it to be true.

If you formulate your perceptions not based on factual evidence that would lead to a false perception and that is exactly what the far left activists groups do. The far left often create paranoia with false perceptions and paranoia has become the far left's greatest weapon. I stated in a previous chapter that information stimulates thought and thought stimulates ideas. To arrive at a logical conclusion the information must be factual or it will create a false perception.

The far left have made some startling accusations regarding

9/11, President Bush, and the United States military. The far left hated former President Bush with such a passion they will accuse him and his administration of any evil deed. Believing their propaganda will inspire more propaganda.

A Rasmussen survey indicated that one out of three

Democrats believed former President George W. Bush had some part in 9/11. Unless the vast majority of the Democratic Party are far-left fanatics, these numbers are staggering. You can dismiss the crazy fringe of the far left because they are wackos with a distorted agenda, but 35% of any group has to include some normal people. If this trend continues it means the Democratic Party is being influenced and taken over by a far left radical fringe. If so, the United States is in for some very rough times.

If people say something long enough and loudly enough they will eventually believe it and influence others to believe it. It does not matter if their information is correct; their persistence and paranoia make it correct. It is like trying to put the round peg in the square hole. As I previously stated, if you get a hammer and pound the round peg long enough and hard enough you can eventually make it fit into the square hole.

Fortunately, most normal, intelligent, and well-read people do not fall for this nonsense. These unproven theories are perpetuated by deranged people, with perverted agendas. Their intentions are cruel and their information is baseless. Most of them will not acknowledge the truth if it is in conflict with their cause. Far-left activist groups thrive on false perceptions.

This type of perception is very dangerous and is very

prevalent in politics. In politics, passions can run very deep and ideology can cause rivals to become very aggressive with each other, almost to the point of hysteria. When two opposing philosophies clash, members of both parties can become verbally combative.

Activist groups supporting a party will look at half- truths and create a smear campaign around them. When this happens, they often attack their opposition and perceive them as a dangerous enemy, even when danger does not exist. They can start to imagine this perceived enemy as much more than a political rival. They often view them as capable of destroying everything they hold dear. Many times their imagination increases their paranoia. I believe this is what has happened with the far left and their perception of former President Bush. They were totally convinced that he represented everything wrong with the world.

This is not a new phenomenon. Take for example the paranoia during the start of World War II and President Franklin D. Roosevelt, whom I consider one of America's great US presidents. It has long been rumored that President Roosevelt was aware of the Japanese intentions to bomb Pearl Harbor. In fact, some have said that FDR actually knew when the attack was most likely to take place and said nothing, because he wanted an excuse to enter World War II.

The notion that any of our presidents would allow our soldiers or our civilians to be murdered without warning is preposterous. I guarantee that the activist groups of that day that opposed FDR were in frenzy and totally convinced of his guilt. They wanted to believe it, so it had to be true.

I believe that some people must create a villain that

they can despise in order for them to feel good about themselves. Obtaining facts means little when arriving at their conclusions. Their entire life has become a false perception. They create a negative perception by continually accusing the same people of the same crimes without any proof. As I said, if you say something or hear something often enough, you might have a tendency to believe it. False perceptions lead to false conclusions.

Example: Creating a perception in the customer's mind is a very effective marketing technique used by national brands when advertising to the consumer. A company like Windex has always told consumers that Windex does not streak. They have told us so often that we buy their product and expect it not to streak. When the product does not meet your expectations it changes your perception. In other words, when you have time to conduct your research by using the product, your perception may change based on factual research.

This is why there is such a controversy on subjects like global warming. There are scientists who agree with the data and scientists who do not. Which scientists are being truthful, and which ones are trying to convince us to fit their agenda? I have become so confused that I do not know what to think.

The problem is, to believe in global warming is politically correct, and that in itself is disconcerting. It has been my experience that the far-left politically correct have agendas, and to further their agendas they sometimes exaggerate the truth. My suggestion on how to uncover the truth is follow the money. Many of these far left global warming crusaders are becoming very wealthy supporting their theory.

Many people share different opinions on this subject. In

fact it was President Reagan that said "Approximately 80% of our air pollution stems from hydrocarbons released by vegetation, so let's not go overboard in setting and enforcing tough emission standards from man made sources." He has credibility with me because he was not seeking a financial reward for his beliefs.

It is like Darwin's theory of evolution versus creation. It is politically correct to believe in Darwin's theory that we all evolved from apes, because it removes religion from the equation. That makes our far-left seculars happy, but is it true? This is a hard subject to research. Evolution means the process of change. Darwin believed in the origin and perpetuation of new species of animals and plants. His theory, as I understand it, is that humans evolved from apes. If it is true, that when one species evolves the other no longer exists, why are there still apes roaming the earth? And where did the apes come from? I have never had anyone answer these questions to my satisfaction.

Most of those who perceive Darwin's theory to be true want it to be true so they have done little research to arrive at their conclusions. They have just heard it so many times that they now believe it. Besides many on the far left are anti-God and Darwin's theory fits into their secular agenda—they want to believe. Perceptions are much easier to perpetuate when you want them to be true.

Another perception in our society is that the United States military has wholesale torture chambers. In fact, some believe that we do not abide by the Geneva Convention and are committing atrocities throughout the world when we capture our enemies. I am sure that these are some of the same people who think our government was responsible for 9/11.

Many people feel that there is never a reason to vigorously interrogate any of our enemies for any reason. As I stated earlier, I refer to these people as the protected. Their perception of our military is that we are the criminals, not our enemy. Usually these people have never had to fight or serve in the military.

When I was in Vietnam, the Vietcong committed many atrocities against American soldiers, and our soldiers returned the favor. Unfortunately, that is how wars are fought in the realistic world. The PC protected live in an idealistic world where they are able to criticize those who protect them without fear of retribution.

The far left perception of our world is, in my opinion, upside down. For example, they believe former President Bush was evil and Fidel Castro was a great leader and humanitarian. They deemed President Bush as politically incorrect in everything he did and gave Castro a pass for his mistakes. They are blinded by their own distorted agenda. I wonder if their perceptions would change if they had to live under a socialist regime. They have the freedom to leave our country at any time. If they decide to leave in favor of a socialist dictatorship like Cuba, I strongly suggest they not voice political dissent against the Cuban government. I am sure if they did their perception of Fidel Castro and his brother the new leader of Cuba would change dramatically.

Perceptions can be very powerful. For instance, the Muslim fundamentalists believe if they commit an act of terrorism in defense of their religion, they will go to heaven and will be surrounded and indulged by a large number of virgins. Christian fundamentalists would view this act of indulgence as lustful sex and equate it to hell. They both cannot be right.

Truth is in the eyes of the beholder.

When your values are based on false perceptions, and hate replaces common sense, your view of the world will become distorted. People who really think that the United States brought down the World Trade Center must be very misinformed, and I am being kind. To continually voice this opinion without proof, makes them sound like lunatics.

Remember, perception is not always truth. Perceptions based on emotions more than on correct information can actually distort the truth. Just because you believe something does not necessarily make it true, as we have seen in this chapter.

Be careful who you listen to and always question their data and motives. Be slow to judge others, encourage diversity of thought, and research before arriving at conclusions. Replace emotion with information and speculation with truth. Stay away from those who are always pointing the finger at others and condemning everyone who does not agree with them. Perceptions should be based on data, not hysteria.

Remember be careful how you formulate your perceptions. You might be wrong. The far-left politically correct never let truth interfere with their perceptions.

CHAPTER 24

The Good, the Bad, the Ugly

This is kind of an interesting chapter, because I could have made this chapter into three chapters. I have always liked to draw comparisons, especially when it involves truth versus deception. Whenever you compare opposites against each other, they expose each other. They both become more obvious.

The good people of this world focus on helping those in need and taking personal responsibility for making the world a better place. The bad focus on meeting an idealistic agenda. They will personally attack anyone who questions that agenda. They continually try to impose a double standard to meet their far left ideology. The ugly are those whose greed and lust for power and money take precedence over humanity. They sell their souls for money and power.

We are going to see how the far-left politically correct play a role in this deception. How their distorted agendas and anti-traditional values undermine our very existence. They will attack any individual or organization that does not conform to their distortion. They attempt to remove normalcy and replace it with confusion. Any traditional values are challenged while perversion is supported.

The three sections of this chapter continue to reflect the theme of this book. When the good, the bad, and the ugly are discussed and compared, it becomes very clear that PC is BS.

223

The good are people who are not interested in furthering their cause or agendas; they are interested only in helping others. In this section, I am going to recognize some people and organizations that do just that—they help make our world a better place. These individuals and organizations are good for our country.

Let us start with the tens of thousands of volunteers who give time and money to help those in need. They volunteer at hospitals, serve on charity boards, and coach Little League teams. They give back to the community because they care about those they serve. They do not seek recognition or personal reward; they just want to help make our society better.

The firefighters from all over the country who volunteered their time to help during our darkest hour after 9/11. While some politicians were laying blame and the far left was accusing our government for the disaster, they did the dirty work in the trenches locating bodies. Many worked seven days a week, twelve hours a day in the worse conditions possible. They risked their lives in dirty, toxic, and unsafe conditions, and as a result some are experiencing health problems today. In fact, there have been at least 57 known deaths attributed to ground zero workers and many firefighters that have been diagnosed with cancer due to their exposure. Knowing the risk, these brave heroes still went to help their comrades in need. They had no agenda other than helping their brethren. Our country owes these men and women a debt of gratitude. They are always there for us. They are our great protectors. We call upon them to do the dirty work and they do so with honor and integrity. They are some of America's best.

The Boy Scouts are a great example of an organization

dedicated to helping our youth. They communicate a positive image to our young boys. It is a worldwide organization that serves boys from eleven to seventeen years old. Founder Lieutenant-General Robert Baden-Powell of Brown Sea Island, England, officially started the Scouts in 1908. The organization was designed to instill character, citizenship, personal fitness, and leadership all the qualities that normal responsible parents would want for their sons. The Boy Scout creed says:

To be trustworthy in all things-loyal, helpful, friendly, courteous and kind To learn obedience and practice cheerfulness and thrift To be brave, clean, and reverent Above all to keep myself physically strong, mentally awake and morally straight To be prepared at all times to do my duty to God and my country and to do a good turn to someone every day.

These are all the qualities that make up good strong character. Therefore, you would think most intelligent, moral, and ethical people would encourage this behavior and applaud this fine organization. You would think educators would adopt this creed and teach it along with their curriculum to ensure character as well as intelligence.

On the contrary Boy Scouts have come under attack recently for not allowing homosexuals in leadership positions. Unfortunately, not all share their values in our politically correct misguided society. The Boy Scout creed has a positive uplifting message that will help build strong character and focuses on giving back.

Many colleges and universities have condemned the Scouts for their stand on the homosexual issue. Case in point—some years ago Syracuse University's former Chancellor Buzz Shaw prohibited the Boy Scouts from having their annual fundraising dinner on the campus of Syracuse University because the Scouts would not allow homosexual scout leaders. Chancellor Shaw had a politically correct agenda and the Boy Scouts did not fit into that agenda.

Can you imagine being penalized for not allowing homosexual leaders in an all-boy organization? If they did allow homosexual leaders to influence and lead eleven to seventeen-year-old boys, they, in my opinion, would be very irresponsible. In our upside down, "wrong is right politically correct society" the Scouts and their ethics and integrity are in question. This type of rationale makes sense only to the far left.

Yet, as previously discussed Boulder High School in Colorado can feature secular speakers who advocate unprotected sex, same-sex relationships, and drug use to our youths and are applauded by the faculty as well as the students. The political far left are trying to force this behavior on our society and pass it off as normal. I will bet you Buzz Shaw would never have outlawed these secular speakers from his campus.

People with the mentality of former Chancellor Shaw are far-left and politically correct. Buzz Shaw penalized the Boy Scouts for upholding the Judeo-Christian traditional values upon which the organization was founded. The Boy Scouts had their values twisted and used against them by those devoid of traditional values.

To me, people with this anti traditional mentality are a disgrace to those they are supposed to be serving. They have a non-traditional secular agenda and view our world through a strange set of glasses. Secular education has preference over morals and character. Far-left secular values are in great conflict with traditional values. Deception and truth are always in conflict with each other.

If the Boy Scouts are going survive as a worthwhile organization, they must stay strong in their convictions. Abe Lincoln said "make sure you put your feet in the right place then stand firm." Their organization stands for what is right, and should never compromise truth for insanity. The Boy Scouts are teaching our youth good principles and building strong character. Both are essential in achieving success. I pray they stay strong in their convictions!

Getting back on point: In this section, I also want to recognize two special individuals who are an inspiration to me because of their dedication, generosity and willingness to go beyond for those in need. I have randomly chosen these people from diverse backgrounds because they are doers not complainers. Recognizing these two may seem peculiar because they are in such different professions. Both are inspirational and have helped many in need, they are the late evangelist Billy Graham and former television talk show host Oprah Winfrey.

Billy Graham was the most famous evangelist in the world. He was born on Nov 7, 1918, outside Charlotte, North Carolina. He was president of Northwestern College from 1948-1952. He founded the Billy Graham Evangelistic Association in 1950.

Billy Graham Crusades were worldwide preaching a message of hope and salvation to millions of the downtrodden.

He has preached Christianity to over 215 million people in 185 countries. His strong principles would not allow him to visit South Africa until apartheid ended. He once paid bail money for Martin Luther King Jr. when Dr. King and his cause were not acceptable to many Americans. Billy Graham was very intelligent and charismatic and could have been successful in many other occupations but instead focused on evangelizing to the world.

Traveling around the world can be exhausting and takes a dedication of purpose and a love for humanity. I applaud his efforts and he has made our world a much better place. Instead of criticizing failed efforts, he has delivered a message of hope and peace. I am sure because of his ethics and morals he was politically incorrect to the PC seculars and that makes him more appealing. Moreover, I would not want it any other way. The good deeds revealed expose bad deeds concealed. If the far-left politically correct approved of Billy Graham I would be worried, but there is no chance of that. Billy Graham, you have done great good for humanity preaching peace, love, morals, and ethics. Thank you.

Oprah Winfrey was born on January 29,1954 in Kosciusko, Mississippi. She attended high school in Nashville, Tennessee. At nineteen years old, she became the nation's youngest television anchor on WTVF-TV in Nashville. In 1984, she moved to Chicago to host a morning talk show, "AM Chicago." After one year it was renamed the Oprah Winfrey Show and remained #1 for twenty plus consecutive seasons.

Oprah is a great humanitarian. She is a true philanthropist. She is always trying to give back. As an employer, she took her entire staff and their families to Hawaii for a week's vacation. That is over 1,000 people. When she invites a guest who is in need to appear on her show, she takes care of that need. Oprah has helped so many people they are too numerous to mention. She has a wonderful intuitive instinct that gives her insight on what to do and how to do it.

She has even given gifts to her studio audience. On one occasion, the entire studio audience received automobiles. I have a sense that giving makes Oprah feel better than those on the receiving end.

Oprah believes that education is the door to freedom. She has awarded millions of dollars toward providing a better education for students who have a desire to learn but no financial means. She gave $40 million to help pupils in Africa complete their education. These young women have a great desire to learn but have the barest essentials to live on. Their reaction and deep appreciation had me in tears.

I do not know her politics and I do not care. Oprah's actions speak much louder than her politics anyway. She never badgers those who disagree with her and therefore I could listen to her regardless of her position. I do know that she is a great person and an inspiration to the entire human race. When it comes to helping those in need, Oprah talks the talk and walks the walk.

The good people and organizations mentioned in this chapter go out of their way to create a better society. Their focus is not to point fingers and accuse others but rather to get personally involved and to help whenever possible. Their passion is to help those in need, and their efforts lead to positive change.

The bad section of this chapter identifies some of the misguided people, organizations, and far-left philosophies that are tearing at the core of our society. Those who have a self-serving distorted ideology will do anything to achieve that agenda. The more vile the attacks on those who do not agree with them, the better they feel. I always look closer at the accuser than those they accuse, especially when they display a hatred for their opposition.

Leading my "bad list" is the now famous Reverend Jeremiah Wright who is, in my opinion, one of our nation's premier racist. He accuses America of racism while preaching a message of hate against the white establishment. Reverend Wright is an abomination to everything good and moral. I believe those that continue to listen to this evil message are either racists themselves or anti-Semitic. Normal fair minded people would exit that "church" as soon as he started preaching that vial message. Being a Christian it embarrasses me when Reverend Wright is referred to as a Christian minister. I call him the evil Reverend Wrong.

Next but not nearly as vial is Nancy Pelosi who's agenda is to secure the Mexican vote by legalizing all illegal immigrants. I know she has not publicly revealed her intentions but I am totally convinced that is her goal. The democrats desperately need the twelve million votes to stay in power and its all about power. She views them as a huge voting block and will do anything including allowing them to break our laws to stay in power.

The National Healthcare Plan that she helped author allows illegal aliens access. This amounts to compromising your ethics, morals and integrity. Selling your principles is the equivalent to selling your soul.

Eric Holder our nation's former attorney general is my next

230

candidate for his mishandling of the Black Panther incident at a voting precinct in Philadelphia during the 2008 national election. Two black panthers were outside the voting precinct armed trying to intimidate voters. Although it is on tape Mr. Holder refuses to prosecute.

Would attorney general Holder have had the same reaction if they had white robes and weapons? If they were Klan members on video tape do you think Mr. Holder would have prosecuted? Creating a double standard only divides our country.

Because of his checker past and Presidential decisions I am adding President Obama to the list because there is an old saying "you don't attract what you want you attract what you are." His association with Reverend Wright for 22 years, his friendship with Bill Ayers, his cabinet appointees, signing a bill with three thousand earmarks and his mishandling of the illegal immigration problem are only the tip of the iceberg. Also his anti-Israel stance and the billions of dollars he gave to Iran sealed the deal for me!

The next group on my bad list is the politically correct protected in our judicial system that is against aggressive interrogation of Islamic prisoners beyond name, rank, and serial number. They focus on the terrorists' civil rights instead of keeping America safe. Our country was built on the rights of our citizens to be free from a dictatorial government. I feel that freedom should be earned and given only to those who are not dedicated to killing our citizens.

I believe we are at war with a dangerous, distorted enemy who will do anything to destroy us. Information is vital to our survival. Gathering important information may take extreme measures. Is the safety of our families worth it? Many PC protected do not think so and are against torture of any kind even if the information would save American lives. It is very easy to adopt this philosophy when you do not have to engage in battle. The PC protected live in an idealistic world that does not deal with reality. They insist that we play fair while our savage enemies break all the rules. As I said, those who let everyone else do their fighting have the luxury to be idealists. They do not have to worry about the consequences of their ideals.

When fighting men and women are interviewed regarding the civil rights of terrorists, they have a completely different opinion. Torture to uncover lifesaving information is perfectly justified by those who have to risk their lives to protect our country. There is an old saying that "you will never meet an atheist in a foxhole." I have another saying—"you will never care about being politically correct in a foxhole" either. Using any and all torture methods to save American lives is acceptable to me. I do not want our enemies killed or maimed when being interrogated, but I do want them very uncomfortable for as long as it takes to get the information needed to save American lives.

In an earlier chapter, I stated that all civil rights for suspected terrorists should be suspended until this crisis is over. Our enemies are ruthless and do not care about the Geneva Convention. They will commit any atrocity to achieve their evil agenda. This does not concern the politically correct idealists, because, as I said, they will never have to fight the enemy in battle. That is the protector's job. Appeasing a brutal enemy does not work. The Nazis taught us that. Torturing potential killers is a necessary evil in war. Instead of worrying about our

Islamic enemies' rights, we had better be concerned about the survival of our democracy.

Mike Nifong also made the bad list for his mishandling of the Duke Lacrosse case. His unscrupulous methods damaged the reputation of three innocent students. They say justice is blind. Well, that certainly applies to prosecutor Mike Nifong. Mr. Nifong did everything he could to convict lacrosse players David Evans, Collin Finnerty, and Reade Seligman. Trying to uncover the truth never entered Nifong's mind. He had already made up his mind regarding their guilt and convicted them, when they were arrested.

Some black groups and black leaders joined the lynching and the racist accusations began. They had already convicted the young men for the simple reason they were white and the young woman in question was black. What hypocrites. Some Duke Professors even joined in the condemnation. It was a politically correct lynching and the far left were rejoicing. These same people are outraged when a minority student is even questioned about a crime, no matter what the evidence indicates.

While doing my research on the Duke case, I came upon a left-wing Web site Blackfeminism.org, and they were so blindly critical of the Duke players that it bordered on insanity. The truth did not coincide with their agenda so they refused to believe it. Their comments included:

- "Athletes and frat boys are more likely to rape than other men."

- "Blatant rich, white, male athletic entitlement."

- "Victims were racially harassed."

- "Most blacks know for sure it was a crime."
- "The victim is a woman of color and a sex worker.

They are going to try very hard to drag her through the dirt. I hope and pray she stays strong."

What racist garbage. I will guarantee you that this racist group is against profiling unless it meets their agenda. The conclusions arrived at by the Website has nothing to do with truth or justice. It has everything to do with justifying a distorted white male racist bias. They do not want equal justice; they want unequal justice tilted in their favor and Mike Nifong almost gave it to them.

The only thing that I felt was more ridiculous than the case itself was the outrage by many criminal defense attorneys toward Mike Nifong's tactics. So because of their outrage they also made my list. I think it is humorous that they were so upset at him for using their tactics, like preventing reliable evidence from entering the courtroom. The criminal defense attorneys call it inadmissible evidence. It is part of the procedural loopholes designed to keep the incriminating truth from the jury so criminals can walk free. I guess it is only morally right when they do it.

Finally, in the Duke case, a just decision was rendered and the three young men were set free. As for Mr. Nifong, the state bar prosecutor said, "Mr. Nifong did not act as a minister of justice, but as a minister of injustice." The committee deliberated ninety minutes and unanimously agreed that Nifong's actions involved "dishonesty, fraud, deceit, and misrepresentation." Michael Nifong was disbarred. In this case, the judicial system finally got it right.

When you have a preconceived agenda based on limited

information, you are running the risk of closing your mind to the truth. Selected information is dangerous because it can strengthen your convictions. The Nazis believed they were the superior race and felt they had to conquer the world to fulfill their agenda. Seeking the real truth was not as important as their perception of the truth. The result was a world conflict and the deaths of millions of people.

I am sure many blog sites and their far-left politically correct ideals, are perpetuated by those who do not have good intentions and realize the damaging consequences of their actions. They do not care whom they hurt as long as they achieve their goals. Guilt and intimidation are their strategy.

I believe the problem is that much of their far-left secular agenda is contrary to our Judeo-Christian values and are harmful to our society. I also believe our traditional values made our country compassionate and prosperous. The elimination of these values in place of a secular nonreligious culture will be destructive.

The ugly are the politicians and corporations that engage in unethical business practices for the sake of greed. Money is the root of their evil. We have our politicians looking into a magnifying glass at their opposition yet overlooking criminal behavior within their own party. Like the case of a Democratic representative who police authorities found with $90,000 in cash hidden in his freezer—his party gave him a committee chairmanship. A Republican politician who had worked for passage of legislation for a corporate "special interest group" was later hired by this group as a lobbyist and was paid millions of dollars. Taking a job as a lobbyist for a corporation that benefited from your political influence may not be criminal, in the judicial sense, but it should be. It is certainly criminal in a moral and ethical sense.

We have corporations cheating their employees out of their pension funds and destroying their companies because of personal greed. CEOs of those companies try to walk away with tens of millions of dollars and leave their dedicated employees with nothing. I can understand why so many people have been disillusioned by big business. Thankfully, most corporations in the United States are honest in their business practices.

Two of the worst examples of corporate greed are Enron and WorldCom. Both of these companies were destroyed by greed. In fifteen years, Enron grew to be the seventh-largest American company. Unfortunately it was built on a house of cards. They lied about profits and concealed their debt. In another words, they cooked the books.

CEO Kenneth Lay, now deceased, and his executive team were urging employees to purchase more stock even when they knew the stock was worthless. Their employees lost billions because their pensions were so heavily invested in Enron's own stock. Talk about immoral and unethical practices. It may also be noted that Enron gave millions of dollars to George W. Bush's 2000 presidential campaign. Large political contributors look for special political favors.

WorldCom—with 85,000 employees and assets of $160 billion—eventually filed for bankruptcy. They were involved in one of the largest accounting scandals in American history. WorldCom stock once traded at $64 per share and dropped to 21¢ per share.

In 2001 the company claimed a $10 billion profit when in reality, from 2000-02, they had a $73 billion loss. They were involved in fraud and misled stockholders, employees, and the public. WorldCom was also built on a house of cards. Their entire strategy was built on hope rather than reality. Their collapse affected the entire industry. As a result, over 300,000 communication employees lost their jobs. What a disgrace and a complete distortion of the truth. It takes corporate immorality to its lowest level. It proves that a thief is a thief regardless of education or social standing.

And saving the best crook for last is Bernie Madoff and his $50 billion ponzi scheme. His company was nothing more than smoke and mirrors and left many of his investors penniless. It is so outrageous and well publicize that it speaks for itself.

A corporation does not have to engage in illegal accounting practices to make my ugly list. They just have to be so horrific in their product development or business practices and demonstrate a complete disregard for humanity. The tobacco industry meets those criteria.

The cigarette companies manufacture a product that addicts and eventually kills their consumers. They have increased the amount of nicotine in their product even after testifying to Congress that they did not. Nicotine is a poisonous alkaloid and very additive. The consumption of this product has burdened our health care system. They are continually allowed to manufacture this product even with documented proof of its affect on society. When we institute our "universal health care" system, it should include banning this product or forcing cigarette manufacturers to subsidize the system.

Here are some alarming statistics by the American Cancer Society (USA):

• One out of every five deaths in our country is related to

smoking.

8.6 six million people are suffering from chronic disease due to smoking.

Secondhand smoke causes 3,400 lung cancer deaths each year in nonsmokers.

• 440,000 people die each year from tobacco use.

• Cigarettes kill more Americans than alcohol, car accidents, suicide, AIDS, and illegal drugs combined.

• Smoking has also been linked to macular degeneration an eye disease that can lead to blindness

Even in Australia, people are adversely affected. A study conducted by the Health Department of Western Australia found among Aborigines, the poorest in Australia, 49% of male deaths and 48% of female deaths are due to smoking. What an awful product, and yet our government still refuses to regulate this product by outlawing the sale of it.

This is one issue I do not blame on the PCs. Our government believes if they mandate cigarette companies to run those silly, how to quit smoking ads, they are doing their part in solving this problem. We as Americans help to pay for the health care of smokers and should be outraged at the legal manufacturing of this product.

Americans should demand that cigarette manufacturers subsidize our health care system instead of allowing them to run those meaningless quite smoking ads. It would demonstrate that their intentions are honorable and not manipulative.

The good do not have an agenda and take personal responsibility in trying to improve the lives of those around them. The bad have a far-left anti-traditional agenda and criticize anyone who disagrees with it. The ugly will do anything for power and money including selling their souls. Let us hope that the good in our society prevail.

CHAPTER 25

Glitz, Glitter, and BS

There was a time when our American traditions were based on recognizing and celebrating good morals and sound ethics. In the past when people gave their word, it was as binding as a signed contract. Parents had a great and positive influence on their families and always had their best welfare in mind when making family decisions. Parents had control of their homes and would accept their children's friends only if they were responsible and respectful. Parents were their children's best role models. Children were always taught to be respectful to all adults including their teachers. Proper attire and courtesy were signs of that respect. Respect was the common denominator that was taught in our homes and society benefited.

Ethics in business were how successful people in business operated. Corporate scandals were the exception not the rule. Good ethics meant that honesty was practiced as the best and only policy. Character meant that you did not lie or cheat anyone for any reason. This was how the average American family and business operated and our society benefited.

Our legal system was founded on truth, which resulted in real justice. The victims were compensated while the criminals were incarcerated. Our streets were safe and we had confidence in our judges and lawyers. It was a time when most of society felt that our justice system was beyond reproach.

Now our society is all about glitz, glitter, and BS. Style has taken over from substance. It is not as important to tell the truth as it is to not being caught when you lie. Now if your crime cannot be proven, you did not commit the crime. A good personality is more important than strong ethics, morals and integrity. The superficial in our society gain prominence and recognition. Hollywood is a prime example of the superficial gaining prominence even when many exhibit little or no character.

Hollywood is the land of make-believe. The problem is they take themselves so seriously. Many far-left Hollywood stars support socialist leaders and their agendas. These socialist leaders are embraced and glorified in Hollywood. These actors are wealthy and celebrate tyrants who deny their citizens freedom of speech. The citizen unfortunate enough to live in these third world countries live in poverty and will do anything to flee their circumstances.

Many involved in the movie industry like Michael Moore are involved in politics and are very combative. They are always accusing politicians, opposed to their point of view, as being out of touch with the masses. Yet they are so superficial that style always takes precedence over character. They are complete phonies because they live in the lap of luxury and endorse socialism.

Whenever Hollywood awards those in their industry it is a lavish affair. The Emmy and Oscar Award ceremony is Hollywood's biggest night and the most important topics discussed are fashion and beauty. If they do happen to refer to politics they are always attacking those that oppose their socialist ideology.

Character and integrity are rarely mentioned yet the far

left are always talking about the importance of truth. Far-left ideology is more about presentation than it is about credibility. What the ideology really amounts to is a lot of BS. They live a luxurious lifestyle and vehemently endorse a socialist ideology for the rest of America.

The criminal element in our society is having a great influence on the young and it is a very negative influence. As previously noted Rap music that glorifies prison life, the raping of women, and the killing of police officers has gained acceptance in our culture and not just the subculture. When those in authority attack this lifestyle they are labeled as racist.

Peer pressure is more important to our youth than family pressure. We see young adults dressing like degenerates and acting even worse. Parents intimidated by their children have stopped parenting. They refuse to address bad behavior and nonperformance to avoid a confrontation.

In our schools, teachers and administrators do not confront bad behavior and, therefore, condone it.

Instead of the good students influencing the bad, it is the other way around. Many students from normal homes try to emulate this third-world subculture. The ridiculous has become acceptable. Good morals are ridiculed and good ethics are considered old fashion. What should we expect when the ghetto culture, which has a great influence on today's youth, considers education a sellout?

Our failing politically correct schools are more interested in appeasing the troublemakers than teaching the serious students. They have lowered their standards and accepted a culture that impedes academic achievement. The message is that it is not cool to try hard in school. School administrators have succumbed to the far-left politically correct BS and that is hurting the performance of our students.

We witness far-left Web sites that have despicable messages of hate and immorality. These people and their messages are horrific. They put those politicians they disagree with in trashy, uncompromising positions by distorting the message and their intentions. Senator Joe Lieberman was a victim of these despicable attacks. A far-left Web site showed a simulation of the senator on his knees in front of then President Bush performing oral sex. What immoral hateful people, just because the senator does not agree with the far left's Iraq policy. These are the worst of the worst in our society posing as patriots. Freedom of speech to the far left consists of censorship and intolerance to all those who disagree with them.

Fair and honest people cannot endorse such immoral and unethical behavior without losing their own credibility. You can always recognize groups with good or bad character by the friends and supporters they attract. Attracting the far left exposes a flawed agenda.

Everything the far-left haters say is a lie and all open-minded Americans will eventually see them for what they are immoral and unethical liars who are incapable of representing the truth. I loathe and disagree with almost everything they stand for. It is immoral and unethical BS and those who endorse it are the problem with America and not those they depict.

What has happened to our society? Why have we compromised our good morals and ethics for junk? Why have the worst in our society had such an influence on the best in our society? I think it all started when our justice and political systems elected to compromise our Judeo-Christian principles for political correctness. They chose to compromise their values by allowing the truth to be distorted.

There was a time when our legal and political systems were considered incorruptible. Maybe it is because we really did not understand how corrupt the process was or maybe we were just so ignorant that we did not realize or want to admit the system was flawed.

We have much more media coverage now and it is harder for these situations to go unnoticed. Their deception is much harder to conceal when the lights are on. Because of this, we are able to witness horrific abuses of the law by those we once trusted and then watch them defend their deception.

I know that I have been very critical of our judges, criminal defense attorneys, and politicians in this book but there is a reason for it. When they commit indiscretions and maneuver their way out of it with questionable tactics, it sends an awful message to the rest of society. It lets society know that crime can pay. They have had a terrible affect on our society and I feel they have contributed greatly to our society's demise.

When I was growing up, I thought that those involved with the judicial and political systems were the most honest people on earth. I think that is the reason I am so critical of them now. I feel that I have been duped because of my ignorance. I was in disbelief when the leaders of the Democratic Party bribed two senators from Louisiana and Nebraska to get the National Healthcare bill passed. I was astonished when they were confronted with their criminal deeds and said "that's how business is done in Washington." These hypocrites will pass judgment on everyone else while absolving themselves of their illegal and immoral activities.

The more I see the more concerned and disillusioned I get. I blame those in Washington for our lost innocence. When Jesus Christ was asked by the people if they should do what the priests and Pharisee's tell them to do he answered "yes do what they say just don't do what they do." Ethics, morals and integrity have been replaced with double-talk and BS.

The far-left ACLU, in my opinion, is the most destructive organization in our country today. They seem to defend those in our society who are against everything traditional. As previously stated the majority of our society is Christian yet the atheists with the far-left ACLU's help removed prayer from public schools. Christian manger scenes are not allowed in public places because of separation of church and state, yet Muslim' religious symbols are allowed. I guess the Muslim religious symbols do not qualify as religious to the biased ACLU.

I am convinced that they hate Christianity, the family structure, and the traditional values that our country was built on. Our Constitution was created to guarantee the rights of all American citizens. We as a democracy are governed by majority rule and should not allow ourselves to be manipulated by the loud perverted minority.

When the family structure is compromised and the parents' authority is minimized the family will become dysfunctional. The family is the foundation upon which our Judeo-Christian values and country was built. I am convinced that the far-left ideology, if unchallenged, will destroy America.

When our schools stop being structured places of learning,

our youth will suffer. When judges and lawyers distort the truth in place of following procedures to benefit the criminal, our streets are less safe. When we condone by our silence and accept a gangster rap culture, our society will pay the price. When our elected politicians lie and cheat, we as a nation become corrupted.

We must not let this pollution continue. The political far left are ruining our country with their anti-traditional agenda. We must not let them continue to break down our family structure. The functional family is the key ingredient to a healthy society. A civilized culture is destroyed from the inside out. Defending our family values is defending our democracy.

In order to get our country moving in the right direction, we must start by defending our traditional morals and ethics. Parents must not give up their parental rights to a bunch of far-left political anti-traditionalists. We must require that all political candidates running for office share our traditional values and are committed enough to defend them. The far left PCs have a distorted, twisted ideology that they are trying to force on the majority and I cannot stress this point enough. We must always challenge this anti-traditional ideology.

Remember, in a democracy the majority rules. Start standing up for your traditional morals and ethics before you lose them. The far left is feeding us nontraditional garbage and we better stop accepting it and stand for what we believe in. Without our strong traditional values, we as a country will cease to exist.

CHAPTER 26

More Phony-Baloney BS

I felt compelled to add this chapter to once again emphasize how politicians, lawyers and activist leaders on the far left and their distorted agendas are ruining America. I did not know whether to include the contents of this chapter in the Racism, Bad behavior, Deception, or Hypocrisy chapters of my book so I added a new chapter. I entitled this chapter More Phony-Baloney, BS so I would remind myself not to get carried away in describing their devious double standards by using inappropriate expletives.

The far left's standard of justice is based on their interpretation of right and wrong, and they change it whenever it is convenient for them to do so. They talk about the importance of justice and demand injustice. They rant and rave about the evils of discrimination and insist on preferential unequal treatment in their favor. They purposely distort the facts to fit into their biased agenda. They will defend this nonsense and will rarely, if ever, admit or apologize for their mistakes. The problem is magnified because they are supported by far left politicians, judges and the ACLU.

Wrong has become right and style has replaced substance. It is more important to look good, than to do good. Activist groups will defend the members of their community even when it is an outrage to do so. They vehemently defend their twisted perverted form of justice.

We witness this type of deception every day and are

becoming immune to it. Here we go again with the NAACP who tried to excuse the criminal behavior of Michael Vick, former quarterback of the Atlanta Falcons who was found guilty of animal cruelty. I am frustrated with this organization's double standards. They are biased robots blinded by their own agenda. Many in this organization came to the aid of Michael Vick, as I previously predicted they would. They tried to defend his actions by minimizing the effects of his criminal behavior. This sends and awful message to those they represent as well as polarizing our society. It divides us as a nation into two separate groups—those who stand for truth and those who distort the truth.

If you question this form of justice, you are accused of racism. This organization is an example of a group that is more interested in who committed the crime than the crime committed. They focus their anger only on those outside their community while always excusing and defending those within. Their point of reference is not on right or wrong; instead, it is focused on black or white. If you are black, you are defended and supported no matter what you are accused of; guilt is irrelevant.

Many of these NAACP members who supported Michael Vick are same ones who accused, tried, and convicted the Duke Lacrosse players merely because they were white. Any group that engages in this type of deception loses credibility and is not an organization to be taken seriously. That is why I always say that biased leadership exacerbates racism instead of eliminating it.

Normal, intelligent people see these tactics for what they are—a distortion of the truth. They are practiced by those whose goal it is to further their biased, racist agenda. If a non-minority is accused of a criminal act, they will keep a watchful eye on the situation, always trying to prove racial disparity in the justice system. They presume someone's guilt or innocence, based on color, while condemning those who do the same.

Those who engage in this distortion will overlook their communities' own actions while always exaggerating the behavior of those outside these communities, always trying to prove a point even when no point exists. They are always ready to accuse others of misdeeds and will aggressively defend themselves and their communities' actions no matter how blatant or bizarre those actions maybe.

They are liars who preach phony-baloney BS. They have become oblivious to the truth and would not know it if it stared them in the face. They have become delusional in their assumptions and yet are rarely confronted with their unethical distortions. As a result, they continue to get away with misrepresenting the truth.

As I previously stated when society hears something long enough and loudly enough they start to believe it.

Many in our society feel guilty for crimes they have never committed. Some even feel that they are guilty of racism simply because they are not in a minority. Our politically correct society would rather have us avoid a confrontation with these activist groups than expose their racial agendas. Guilt can be a very effective tool in silencing a majority.

I have never heard these leaders apologize for their actions. They will, in fact, continue to distort the truth, even when it is revealed to them, that their allegations are false.

Remember Al Sharpton's defense of Tawanna Brawley

and her allegations of rape. "Reverend" Sharpton has never apologized for his actions even though the allegations were complete BS. Yet he made a huge issue and demanded an apology from Imus when he made his disparaging remarks regarding the Rutgers women's basketball players. In stead of being vilified Mr Sharpton has even been given his own show on NBC. What a disgrace!

I worked for an NBC affiliate in Syracuse, New York for many years and thought the program director would base their programing on their ability to reach a large audience and that the program was credible. In my opinion watching a fraud like Al Sharpton does neither. No wonder they are losing market share!

These false leaders are encouraged and defended by the rest of the far-left PCs because any attack on the establishment is welcomed and acceptable. Many legitimate leaders do not have the courage to stand up and condemn these biased leaders for fear of reprisal. As a result, the ridiculous has become acceptable.

The NAACP has successfully convinced the NFL to reinstate Michael Vick now that he has served his sentence. The Atlanta chapter's former president of the NAACP, Dr. R. L. White, made a statement in support of Michael Vick saying that he would get better treatment if he were a murderer. That is phony BS and he knows it. There they go, claiming to be victims of the system while they continue to extort it. He went on to say that, he does not support dog fighting and compared it to hunting. It is a ridiculous comparison because hunters kill their prey quickly, trying to prevent suffering, and the people who engage in dog fighting make a living betting on which dog will destroy the other dog and continually fight the dogs to inflict more pain and suffering.

Vick and his group even took it one step further by brutally destroying the dogs that did not perform well by massacring them in the most horrific ways possible. No, these are not sportsmen; these are thugs who get a thrill out of destroying animals. To compare them to hunters is like comparing the Boy Scouts with Al-Qaeda.

Dr. White is dedicated to excusing criminal behavior if those committing the crime are the right color. What biased phony BS. How can anyone call this organization or Dr. White credible? I wonder what he thought of the Pete Rose situation. Pete Rose, a former professional baseball player and Michael Vick were caught gambling in violation of their respective sports. I will bet he is not nearly as forgiving in the Pete Rose case. Racists will always be able to explain the difference.

Dr. White and the NAACP are a great example of an organization that changes its standards when it is convenient to do so. If they could get away with it, I am sure they would try to blame the dogs for Mr. Vick's problems.

Dr. White is perfect for his position because he does not want justice; as I said, he insists on injustice and tries to intimidate society to achieve it. I take my hat off to those leaders in the black community who condemned the subhuman behavior of Michael Vick and his dog fighting friends. They are credible without compromise.

I always told my son that I would die for him but he had better never ask me to lie for him. Excusing and defending criminal behavior creates a destructive lifestyle that affects an entire community. We witnessed in the bad behavior section of this book how excusing bad behavior can have horrible consequences.

Dr. White went on to say that he agreed with Vick's decision to accept a plea bargain if it's in his best interest, but he questioned the credibility of Vick's co-defendants, saying an admission of guilt might be more about cutting his losses than telling the truth. Could Dr. White be inferring that Michael Vick was not as guilty as the evidence indicates?

Dr. White and the NAACP are why I added this chapter to my book—to expose him, his organization and people like him for their smoke-and-mirrors-type mentality. I am sure it does not even make sense to them, but it earns them points in their community. It is phony-baloney BS at its lowest level.

How does Dr. White explain the many dog shelters on Mr. Vick's property? How does he explain that all the dogs in question were pit bulls? How did the dogs get there? How did the dogs involved get all chewed up? Why would Vick's co-defendants agree to a plea unless the evidence was overwhelming?

I grew up in the inner city and the inner-city guys are tougher than most and would not roll over on their friends unless they thought it was futile to continue to deny the truth. Mr. Vick was caught dead to rights or he would not have agreed to a plea bargain, and neither would his lawyers.

We have seen in previous chapters how the criminal defense attorneys love to manipulate the system to the benefit of the criminals they represent. There must have been overwhelming evidence for them not to take their chances in court and yet Dr. White is still skeptical.

I think if he actually attended the dogfights, he would still be in denial. He would probably still blame Mr. Vick's problems on our racist society or the dogs. Shifting the blame is a very effective strategy to avoid personnel responsibility.

The NAACP is dedicated to identifying and exposing racism. They have made a lucrative career on their ability to do so. They will attempt to make any situation look racist. I would venture that they would be able to make a case for racism even if Obama won the presidential election one hundred million votes to one. Their outrage would focus on the one that did not vote for him, even though most black candidates will receive 95% of the black vote in most elections.

This type of double-standard racist injustice encourages more outlandish behavior. In Louisiana, six black teenagers violently attacked a white teenager Justin Barker and beat him senseless. They beat him because he is white. This incident was referred to as the Jena Six trial, and instead of condemning the actions of these six teenagers, many black leaders were protesting and defending them. Those who defend this injustice are so blatantly racist that they are oblivious to their own distorted ideology.

These phony leaders focused on the charges against the six, rather than the crime. It is again an example of these racists changing their criteria of justice to justify their double standards. If six white teenagers beat a black teenager, they would then switch their criteria back to justify their outrage. They are phony make-believe leaders who mislead and distort the truth whenever it is necessary to do so. The problem is, leaders who engage in these tactics destroy their communities and blame everyone else when this happens.

Allowing this type of leadership to go unchallenged has

caused a big problem with other activist groups. We now have many of these groups demanding special rights above and beyond, what the rest of society is entitled to. Again, the majority remains silent rather than confront this double-standard phony baloney BS.

Whenever activists with non-traditional agendas are not challenged, it gives them a feeling of empowerment. They start to feel that their demands are reasonable and this encourages more outrageous demands. It also encourages other groups to follow their lead. Moral and ethical people should be our society's idea of a role model, not the thugs and misfits.

Many Arab-American groups are now filing lawsuits and threatening anyone engaged in profiling even when it is in our country's best interest to do so. Illegal immigrants demonstrate in the streets of America demanding their citizenship even though they have broken our laws by illegally entering our country. Many in politics cheat and steal to achieve their agendas and are rarely held accountable. People from both parties engage in unethical practices and this is sending a negative image to our nation's most impressionable. Secular non-religious far-left groups try to impose their anti-traditional agendas and have been successful in changing our sacred traditions. Yet the majority of our society remains silent.

It is a shame that it has come to this because organizations like the National Association for the Advancement of Colored People (NAACP) founded in 1909 was a great and necessary organization with a wonderful history. It was dedicated to fighting and eradicating discrimination in our country and had a positive impact. Unfortunately, in their enthusiasm to fight injustice for one group, they have created injustice for another.

Whenever you favor a group based on color to the exclusion of another, you are engaging in discrimination. None should understand this more than the NAACP.

To regain their credibility I propose a name change for the NAACP to the NAAHR (National Association for the Advancement of the Human Race) dedicated to helping all victims of discrimination instead of helping people of color escape justice. Besides, we already have a criminal rights group, the ACLU.

I predict if the NAACP did this they could once again regain their credibility and be embraced by an entire nation. I am for any organization that helps those in need as long as they are fair and unbiased. When you are blindly dedicated to one group and as a result penalize another that is phony-baloney BS.

CHAPTER 27

The Interview

Some years ago I had a great opportunity to interview a wonderful man from Caracas, Venezuela,

Mr. Eddy Martinez. Mr. Martinez is a Venezuelan citizen who was seeking asylum in the United States because of the Hugo Chavez regime. He graduated from Zulia University with a degree in mechanical engineering. He worked at the PDVSA (Petroleos De Venezuela, Sociedad Anonima) oil company in Venezuela for twenty-seven years as a mechanical engineer and as a specialist in business administration. During his employment, he served in corporate management of integrated services in gas compression.

Eddy is the cousin of Orlando Ferrer, my friend and former neighbor. In fact, Orlando, his wife Susan, and their son Orlando, Eddy and his daughter Racquel are some of the nicest people my wife and I have had the pleasure to meet in Florida. I was eager to include this chapter in my book to finally uncover the truth about the Chavez presidency.

We all have witnessed people like Danny Glover,

Don King, Sean Penn and others who embrace Chavez and sing his praises as a great leader. I know Glover and Penn are on the far left and not exactly geniuses but I figure they must have done some research and have insight into this man and his politics for them to be so supportive.

Many of these entertainers are huge fans of Chavez and considered former President Bush the real enemy to our civilization. Many in Hollywood hated President Bush, yet seemed mesmerized by President Chavez and I had to find out why.

People like Danny Glover and Sean Penn as I said are on the far left and are usually involved with causes that I find hard to embrace but I wanted to give them the benefit of the doubt. In the past, I have not been fans of the far left in Hollywood because I have felt they tell us how to live and are unable to run their own lives successfully. Their minds are closed and they are combative toward anyone who disagrees with them.

I did not want to follow suit so I needed to open my mind to the possibility that I may have misjudged this Chavez situation. To me, President Chavez on the surface seems like nothing more than a Fidel Castro wannabe. Is he a liberator or, like his counterpart Fidel, a tyrant? To find out I had to go to the source and had the opportunity to interview a citizen of Venezuela and get the real story. Eddy Martinez was kind enough to engage me. I knew firsthand that Eddy was seeking asylum so I was not surprised to find out that he was not a big fan of President Chavez. I have also found him to very credible in every situation so I still felt very comfortable in interviewing him. I wanted to know the reason why he was leaving his beloved homeland and his opinion on Hugo Chavez. I had this interview in 2006 prior to President Bush leaving office.

* * *

The following is a candid interview with Mr. Martinez:

What is it like to live in Venezuela?

The Venezuelan people are a warm, kind, and happy people. The family and family values are very important. In most families, regardless of their financial situation, everyone takes care of each other. There is class distinction regarding wealth but everyone gets along. Prior to Chavez taking over in 1998 we had a democracy with all our freedoms. Those freedoms have been slowly eroding and life is not the same.

I am a lifelong resident of Venezuela and only want to leave my beloved country because of Chavez. He is ruining the private health system to gain favor with the poor. Education prior to Chavez was very good and it required a great deal of study to achieve a certified education. Now, education is being negatively affected by the government, because they are eliminating all tests required for college entry. Everyone can go to college regardless of academic achievement. College degrees are given not earned and, therefore, many of those receiving degrees are not qualified. A revolution thrives on ignorance.

What is the main difference between the United States and Venezuela?

The people of Venezuela, as a whole, are much warmer and friendlier, than even those in the United States, but Americans respect the laws more than the Venezuelans do. Freedom in the United States is taken for granted. I am not a President Bush lover; in fact, I don't care much for him but the amazing thing about this country is you can voice your disapproval of your president without fear of reprisal. In Venezuela, you do not dare to oppose Chavez.

If you are a Chavistas (Chavez loyalist) the government will guarantee your freedoms. You ensure your freedoms only by being a loyal follower of Chavez. If you openly voice your disapproval of Chavez, you become an enemy of the revolution and will lose your freedoms. In essence, you have to buy your freedom by keeping your mouth shut. Americans take for granted their freedom of speech. It is a great country because you can say what you want without fear of retaliation. If you dare talk negatively in Venezuela about the government, you are considered a traitor, the enemy, and will be prosecuted. I cannot stress this difference in the two countries enough. Freedom of the press in Venezuela consists of being able to criticize any other government in the world but not the Venezuelan government under his leadership. He continues to discourage political dissent.

Why then do you think actors like Danny Glover, Sean Penn and others in Hollywood speak so highly of Hugo Chavez?

I do not know for sure. Maybe they have a socialistic preference. Also, it is well known in my country that Danny Glover received lots of money ($20,000,000) from Chavez for preparing a movie. When these celebrities visit my country, they stay at the presidential plaza in beautiful surroundings and see Venezuela through tainted glasses. They are wined and dined. Living in a country and being entertained in a country is completely different. I cannot really tell you what their attraction to Chavez is. I am only guessing. They certainly see him a lot differently than most others in Venezuela.

Can you leave and return to Venezuela whenever you want?

Yes, you can, but only if you do not criticize the government. You are considered a security threat if you make anti-government statements. We are not like the United States where citizens can say what they think when they think it. Those who have opposed the government have had to leave the country and gain asylum first before speaking out against Chavez. If not, they would be put in jail for their anti-government speeches. Chavez is above the law and above criticism. I am doing this interview with you because you assured me that the book would not be published before I gained political asylum.

I know you do not like President Bush or President Chavez, but what is the difference between the two, as you see it?

George Bush has to share his power and cannot become an absolute ruler of his people; Chavez can. America has put safeguards into their democracy to prevent any president from taking over the government. I know some in your country become paranoid about losing their civil liberties but they have no idea what that is really like living outside America. Also, when your president makes a mistake, Americans can feel free to criticize him. You cannot with Chavez and I do not care who says you can, because they are wrong. I am a lifelong resident of Venezuela and believe me you cannot compare the two governments. One is the president of a country and the other is a dictator trying to hide the fact that he is a tyrant. If Bush wanted to be a dictator, as I said, your government has safeguards to prevent that from happening. We apparently do not.

Why did you leave your job at the PDVSA oil company after twenty-seven years?

Because I felt that the practices of the company were being compromised and I did not swear allegiance to the government of Hugo Chavez. Chavez became president in 1998 and in four years, I witnessed a change in policy as well as personnel. The Chavez government fired over 20,000 qualified oil production specialists and replaced them with Chavistas, loyalists. The company was giving into political pressure and advancement was determined on your politics not on your ability. When you were interviewed at work, you were asked about your political affiliation with the government. If you were pro government you were eligible for hire or advancement; if not, you were replaced.

You seem to still have a real love for Venezuela, why not try to stay and change your country instead of leaving it?

I feel at risk remaining in my country. I think it would be just a matter of time before my government would find an excuse to throw me in prison. In fact, the government has started legal proceedings against me for trying to receive my retirement package. At first I was told I would receive my retirement package; now they are accusing me of job abandonment and sabotaging the government and company. If I do not leave, I feel I will eventually be put in jail. Either way, my retirement has been taken away from me.

What do you think will be the future for Venezuela?

I do not see a future for me or my family in my country. My country is becoming a scary place to live. For instance, every child is required to be well versed in the use of firearms. Private property is at risk as a result of his socialist agenda. If the government decides to take your home, they can. They can also move another family into your home at any time. I also believe that Venezuela will become another Cuba. It will become another poor socialist country. Where the president and the government share the majority of the wealth and the people become disenfranchised. What I find amusing is that many of the Venezuelan government officials who criticize George Bush and America have homes in Florida. They speak out of both sides of their mouths.

Is there anything more you would like to comment on?

Yes, the Chavez government is corrupt in many areas. For example, the government figures state that my previous company, PDVSA oil production, is at 3,400,000 barrels of oil per day. Documentation from all other sources disputes these figures as inflated. OPEC and other international energy companies put the figures at 2,400,000 barrels per day. The government is inflating the figures to demonstrate their efficiency to the people. The shame of it is that our company (PDVSA) was projected, in our business plan, prior to the firings, to do over 6,000,000 barrels per day by the year 2007. Now they have to inflate the figures to 3,400,000, well below our projected estimates just to make it look like oil production is more efficient with them in charge. The company has not grown in the last nine years. PDVSA in the 1990s was valued, by industry experts, at the same level as Exxon and Mobil, before their merger. Now because of corruption and mismanagement by the government, they have dropped to the level of a third-world country. It is complete deception and mismanagement.

A dictator always has to have an enemy to create passion among his followers. It also helps them to have a scapegoat to blame their problems on and divert responsibility. Cuba and Venezuela's scapegoat is the United States, especially President Bush. He has become their hated enemy. They portray President Bush as evil, yet Chavez has aligned himself with the presidents of Iran, Syria, and Libya, the real evil of the

265

world. Evil attracts evil.

It is easy to gain loyalty from those who have little, especially if they are ignorant. Any type of change for them is better than what they currently have. There is a saying in Spanish that says, "Por La Plata baila el mono," which means by the money the monkey dance. With his money, Chavez is trying to make the people of Venezuela blindly follow him by distorting the truth.

* * *

After doing this interview with a citizen of Venezuela, I more than ever wondered why some of the far-left elite who embrace Chavez are doing so. Are they trying to overlook the bad that he does because they see so much of the good? Or are they just so anti President Bush that they will side with anyone who calls the president their enemy? I am confused because I know there are many more like Eddy Martinez in Venezuela. If people are interested in finding out the truth, they should do lots of research and get different perspectives from intelligent sources.

I want to thank my new friend Eddy for agreeing to do this interview and for being so candid. I think my definition of the far-left elite may be correct, lots of money, little in the way of research and a great need to hate those with whom they disagree. Far-left political activism is BS.

Epilogue

As you have just read, I am neither far left nor politically correct. I do not believe in worrying about defending the civil rights of terrorists. I believe that the police should be allowed to use as much force as necessary to apprehend dangerous criminals who are resisting arrest. I believe the meaning of political correctness is to implement a double standard that gives an unfair advantage to a minority. I believe in profiling and wiretapping to avoid a national disaster. I believe that truth should always take precedence over procedures. I believe that our judicial system is broken and favors the criminal.

In my book PC is BS I have tried to be very candid on the state of America. I blame most of our nation's problems on a far-left ideology. I also blame the judges, lawyers, and politicians who have given into this ideology. Most politicians are lawyers and are products of the judicial system's procedural mentality, a mentality that is more interested in the process than the truth.

I believe terrorists are evil and inflict great harm on the innocent. They are deranged, because they do this evil in the name of their God. They are impossible to negotiate with and use every method possible to carry out their diabolical terror. This includes sacrificing their own children. Allowing them to manipulate our judicial system puts all of us at risk. When dealing with this evil element, we should use our advanced technology first and worry about their civil rights later. Keeping America safe should always be our top priority.

I believe profiling is unfortunate but necessary in our post-9/11 world. We have seen firsthand the horrific consequences of not being diligent. We must be able to identify the enemy and always be prepared. Muslim fundamentalists have made their intentions very clear and we should be proactive in our response. Evil fanaticism should be met with strength and force instead of procedures. Force is the only thing evil understands.

I believe we can ensure civil rights only when the truth is revealed. Allowing loophole-savvy lawyers to manipulate our criminal justice system ensures injustice. This is not protecting individual rights; it is encouraging individual abuse. It is injustice when criminals avoid prosecution.

I believe that our judicial system is unjust. The judicial system was designed by lawyers, and is, therefore, complicated and confusing. Following procedures becomes much more important than uncovering the truth and fixing the problem. Lawyers are evaluated on their ability to manipulate the system. This manipulation by criminal defense attorneys to exonerate their guilty clients is especially dangerous when terrorism is involved. This allows terrorists to escape justice and continue to randomly plot and carry out their acts of terror. Our judicial procedural system is putting all of us in great danger.

In the aftermath of 9/11, our national leaders still cannot come together on border security. This puts our society at great risk and ensures another eventual terrorist attack. It has been recently revealed that Hezbollah is at our southern border plotting their next intrusion against the American people. When I heard this I was not surprised. The only people surprised by this would have to be our "brilliant" politicians.

The far-left ACLU challenges the profiling of suspected

terrorists even when it makes complete sense to profile. The safety of our country depends on it. The ACLU disguises itself as a defender of civil rights when they are actually an offender of victim rights. They are so anti-traditional in their values that they cannot hide their bias.

Wrong has become right and right has become wrong, especially when opposing traditional values. The far left will come to the defense of radical speakers who endorse non-traditional sexual behavior and the use of illegal drugs, even when this message is being given to children. They will also oppose any speaker who endorses prayer in school because of separation of church and state. Which message is more beneficial to young adults, indiscriminate sex and drugs or abstinence, prayer, and clean living?

The far left in our country are very loud and aggressive and try to intimidate all those who do not agree with them. They always claim they endorse freedom of speech and shout down anyone with an opposing point of view. They do not endorse free speech; they endorse only far-left politically correct speech, which amounts to censorship.

While doing my research, I have found that the ACLU, many criminal defense attorneys, judges, and politicians support the far left. In fact, it is very hard to tell them all apart. Most support a far-left politically correct agenda because, the more confusing they can make the laws, the more we need them to bring their form of clarity. When our nation is in turmoil, they look around at who is to blame and never take responsibility for their actions. They are the reason for our country's problems.

Responsible clear-thinking Americans, with strong family

values, better wake up and stop being intimidated by the radical element of our society. In the past, we have always corrected our mistakes concerning civil rights, women's rights, and freedom of speech. Our country was built on Judeo-Christian values, and we should defend those values and not be made to feel guilty by those without values.

We allow political dissent and freedom of religion, unlike the Islamic fundamentalists who murder their opposition. We are a great country and should recognize and be ready to defend what made us great. **Our Constitution and Judeo-Christian principles are the main reason our country has been the world leader and the reason people from all over the world come to America! To allow any group to change or eliminate these values will become our eventual downfall!**

As you have read I am very candid regarding who I believe is ruining America. I describe how keeping silent when the far left try to impose their distorted agenda amounts to condoning that perversion. In a democracy, we the people have the right to disagree with those who do not engage in moral and ethical behavior. Truth should always be our litmus test for our laws and for those whom we elect to uphold them. We have a right and an obligation to demand that our politicians and judges are honest and trustworthy in the decisions they render.

When any group tries to force their lifestyle on society, we must be very diligent to judge their intentions as well as their agendas. Americans are allowing a dysfunctional minority to impose their secular non-traditional values on the majority in place of our Judeo-Christian values. Beware, because nontraditional values amount to no values.

The biggest problem I have with the far-left political agenda is that it is without long-term solutions and usually favors one group to the exclusion of another. It just does not work because most of their philosophy is based on idealism and not realism.

Now that I have completed my book and had a chance to reflect on my thoughts I now know why President Obama and his administration frightened me. I have discussed throughout my book that far left activists, lawyers and politicians are at the root of our country's eventual demise. Former President Obama was all three; a far left activist, lawyer and politician.

America could not have chosen a leader with a more idealistic far left ideology and with zero business experience. Couple that with his involvement in Chicago politics. As his presidency is still being evaluated and this remains to be seen I feel America under Obama set us back many years as a Christian nation. Remember, PC is BS.

The political left's mentor Saul Alinski dedicated his book: Rules for Radicals to Lucifer! That's why the political left are so violent! Alinski's philosophies promote violence and are completely against our Judeo-Christian beliefs which have made America the envy of the world!

That's why I wrote Political Correctness is BS!

Author's Observations

How come most career politicians who made between $125,000-175,000 a year are worth tens of millions of dollars when they leave office? How were they able to accumulate such wealth?

To clarify my first observation: Remember when President Obama's U.S. Senate seat ($175,000 yearly) was available and someone offered $5,000,000 to buy it. If politics were legitimate it would take almost 40 years to get back their initial investment. I think they must know something the rest of us don't know!

I believe many Republican politicians have a misguided sense of security. They believe that the voters want a change in leadership in Washington when in reality they want to change how government operates.

Washington has become completely dysfunctional because most of our elected officials are lawyers. Lawyers are processed focused and therefore love complexity. They practice manipulation and distortion when arriving at their conclusions. That is why illegal immigration is not enforced. Our laws state that it is against the law to enter our country illegally and our "fearless" leaders in Washington will not enforce the law. They have manipulated truth to fit their political agenda. This is the same agenda that justified giving hundreds of million of dollars in bribes to pass the

National Healthcare Bill. They cheat, lie and steal in the name of politics and are ready to condemn those on Wall Street for less.

The problem is exacerbated with their judicial mentality.

Procedures have replaced truth and common sense has become uncommon. Politicians/lawyers will always justify this distortion and condemn those that question these methods. Organizations like the ACLU make a mockery of traditional truth and justice. They are our nation's worst enemy. They have manipulated our Constitution by defending the rights of the criminal to the detriment of the victim.

Capitol Hill is referred to as the "Last Plantation" by Washington insiders. Can anyone argue with that analysis? Our politicians/lawyers are ruining our country and becoming wealthy in their efforts.

The Tea Party has succeeded in bringing this criminal behavior to the forefront. Term limits should become law and the Congress should not be allowed to pass anything for the American people that they themselves do not participate in. **Our Constitution is America's perfect blue print and it is being marginalized. "We the people are the rightful masters of both Congress and the courts, not to overthrow the Constitution but to overthrow the men who pervert the Constitution." Abe Lincoln**

AUTHORS BIO:

I spent my career in sales and sales management and was fortunate enough to work for WSYR, an NBC affiliate located in Syracuse, New York. Over my career we were owned by S.I. Newhouse, later Katz Communication and then employee owned by New City Communications. All great companies are dedicated to their employee's growth and success and they were!

They provided us the best corporate trainers in the world. Example-Herb Cohen, who negotiated with Iran for the release of our embassy personal, trained us in negotiations. At the time he was considered the best negotiator in the world!

After leaving the media business, with my expertise in hand, I became a Corporate Leadership, Sales and Marketing Consultant with clients in the U.S. and Australia! My previous book: Create Loyal Customers in an Unl-oyal World describes my leadership, sales and marketing system from beginning to end in its exact order. I have always believed that great companies emulate the functional family. The functional family is the most efficient and effective group ever! Because they love, teach and discipline those they lead.

Many years ago I created 5 elements that would enable leaders to become role models and a great resource to those they lead: Below is my definition of great and effective leadership!

• **Role models** -Great leaders will never ask those they lead to do anything they themselves won't do. If they do they will lose all credibility and anything they say after that will be questioned. Role models are always on time, well dressed with a positive attitude. They lead by example!

• **Improve the Skills and Behavior of those they lead** - They never blame others when their team is not successful. These leaders are always looking to improve the skills of those they lead. Never resting on their previous achievements or blaming others for their mistakes!

• **Discipline non-performance** - to improve performance. Their goal is to improve the individual and team performance. To become great you must continually improve and set and meet high standards and expectations. Mistakes have to be identified and corrected.

• **Motivate through recognition** - because great leaders have to discipline nonperformance they much recognize and celebrate a job well done. If leaders only find fault they will drain their team of its energy! I always recommend great achievement should be celebrated as a team!

• **Strategists** - are always getting together as a team and reviewing successes and failures with the ultimate goal of improving performance. Never content with being the market leader!

Sun Tzu said: "It is that in war that the <u>victorious strategist</u> only seeks battle after victory has been won."

• 1963-1965 Attended Onondaga Community College Syracuse, NY

• 1966 Parsons College Fairfield Iowa. January enrollment (Basketball Scholarship)

• September 1966 Drafted

• 1967-68 Military service Vietnam

• 1968 Started career in Broadcast sales

• 1971 joined NBC affiliate WSYR A/F sales staff Syracuse, New York

• 1978 became General Sales Manager 17% revenue share in a 21 station market

• 1982 sales team increased revenue share to 40%

• 1986 Revenue share 55% #1 in USA

• 1992 Created Step2 Training Systems-Corporate, Leadership, Sales and Marketing Consultant (US & Australia)

• Author of 3 books: Political Correctness is BS Mouth Off & Create Loyal Customers in an Un-loyal World

• October 6, 2013 Age 70 completed 630 Chin-Ups in 2 hours 12 minutes 19 seconds World Record (not associated with Guinness)

Made in the USA
Lexington, KY
28 November 2019

57777513R00166